The
WORST-CASE SCENARIO
Survival Handbook:
LIFE

The
WORST-CASE SCENARIO
Survival Handbook:
LIFE

By Joshua Piven and David Borgenicht
Illustrations by Brenda Brown

CHRONICLE BOOKS
SAN FRANCISCO

Library of Congress Cataloging-in-Publication Data available.

ISBN 10: 0-8118-5313-6
ISBN 13: 978-0-8118-5313-2

Manufactured in Canada

Typeset in Adobe Caslon, Bundesbahn Pi, and Zapf Dingbats

Additional research and writing by Piers Marchant

Designed by Frances J. Soo Ping Chow
Illustrations by Brenda Brown

Visit www.worstcasescenarios.com

Distributed in Canada by Raincoast Books
9050 Shaughnessy Street
Vancouver, British Columbia V6P 6E5

10 9 8 7 6 5 4 3 2 1

Chronicle Books LLC
85 Second Street
San Francisco, California 94105
www.chroniclebooks.com

WARNING

When a life is imperiled or a dire situation is at hand, safe alternatives may not exist. To deal with the worst-case scenarios presented in this book, we highly recommend—insist, actually—that the best course of action is to consult a professionally trained expert. But because highly trained professionals may not always be available when the safety or sanity of individuals is at risk, we have asked experts on various subjects to describe the techniques they might employ in these emergency situations. THE PUBLISHER, AUTHORS, AND EXPERTS DISCLAIM ANY LIABILITY from any injury that may result from the use, proper or improper, of the information contained in this book. All the answers in this book come from experts in the situation at hand, but we do not guarantee that the information contained herein is complete, safe, or accurate, nor should it be considered a substitute for your good judgment or common sense. And finally, nothing in this book should be construed or interpreted to infringe on the rights of other persons or to violate criminal statutes; we urge you to obey all laws and respect all rights, including property rights, of others.

—The Authors

CONTENTS

Trouble is the common denominator of living.
It is the great equalizer.

—Søren Kierkegaard

It's always somethin'. If it ain't one thing,
it's another.

—Roseanne Roseannadanna

INTRODUCTION

It's just the way life is—a series of unpredictable occurrences you can't control. And no matter how hard you try to prepare, no matter how many supplies you store, no matter how many plans you make, the unexpected always seems to be the only thing you can ever really expect.

Yet we continue to think we can nail things down, count on them staying the way they are, and then improve on them so we can have a better time and a nicer future. This tendency has been a characteristic of humankind since the dawn of man. We have always sought to build a better Mammoth-trap. All of our greatest discoveries and inventions, even the accidental ones, came from this uniquely human desire to figure out a better way to do things so we can reap the benefits. Fire, tools, the wheel, and domesticating animals, for example, were supposed to improve the life of early humans.

But what people consistently failed to take into account was that every invention or improvement, every decision or action, opens up a whole new range of unexpected possibilities on top of the old unexpected possibilities. Not only can't you plan on the old way to be dependable and safe, you now have new things that can go wrong, too. More eventualities to prepare for. In every aspect of life.

How is mankind to deal with these spiraling, ever-increasing risks?

The book you hold in your hands, *The Worst-Case Scenario Survival Handbook: Life,* is the answer.

This amazing book provides instant answers to more than 600 of daily life's sudden turns for the worse. There you are, minding your own business, walking down the street when *POW!* you get a severe case of hiccups, or are chased by a pack of dogs, or realize you've run into someone who has taken an overdose of aphrodisiacs, or you see a cat stuck in a tree—the list of problems is endless. In this book, you'll learn the one sure thing to do in the widest array of subjects yet tackled by the *Worst Case Scenario Survival Handbook* series. All areas of life are covered, with chapters on Health, Beauty & Fitness, Home, Pets, Sports & Hobbies, Jobs, Travel, Food & Cooking, and the Stages of Life from childhood to old age; from minor injuries to major ailments and fixing the kitchen sink. This may well be the only book that gives you the hands-on, practical advice to save your life, your marriage, your house, your dog, your job, *and* your dinner party.

Search by subject or in the index in the back to address a pressing problem, or read a little bit every day to bone up on your survival skills. There's not a single page here that wouldn't make you better prepared for the surprises that life brings.

As before, all the answers within come from experts in the subject at hand—doctors, beauticians, survival experts, sports therapists, psychologists, stunt people, FBI agents—people from all walks of life who have experienced the worst and lived to tell about it.

You can't control the uncontrollable, but you can be better prepared to deal with what comes. Never be complacent, always be vigilant. Look for new scenarios and updates on www.worstcasescenarios.com, and let us know what situations you encounter that are not in this book.

We have to help each other out. It's a jungle out there, right in your own backyard.

—The Authors

CHAPTER 1
HEALTH

HYGIENE

Rusty Razor Blade

Soak the razor blade in white vinegar or cola overnight, then sterilize the blade by rubbing it with a cotton ball steeped in rubbing alcohol.

Toothbrush Falls in Toilet

Scrub and soak the brush in hydrogen peroxide. Place in boiling water for 5 minutes. Replace the toothbrush at first opportunity.

No Toothbrush

Moisten a sheet of paper towel or tissue with water and use a kneading motion to work along the surfaces of your top and bottom teeth with your fingers. Inspect your teeth in the mirror to be sure all buildup has been removed. Scrape your tongue by moving your top row of teeth across it from back to front several times. Rinse your mouth thoroughly with water.

Emergency Toothpick

Edges of business cards, paperback or matchbook covers, menus, envelopes, a piece of paper folded into quarters, plastic-tipped shoelace ends, or CD jewel case corners may all serve as emergency toothpicks. Avoid using paper-clips, pins, ballpoint pen nibs, or any other metal object.

FILTHY HOTEL ROOM

Do not come into direct contact with red hazard areas.

"Furry" Tongue

Scrape the top of your tongue with the edge of an upside-down teaspoon to remove bacteria buildup. Place a small amount of antiseptic mouthwash in your mouth and brush your tongue and teeth for several minutes, then rinse. Brush your teeth and tongue with fluoride toothpaste.

Public Transportation

Sit as close to a door as possible to be near fresh air as it enters the bus or train car. If there are no seats available, maintain your balance with a wide stance. Wear gloves or encase your hands in a scarf to hold on to the bar or strap rather than using your bare hands.

Grimy Toilet in Public Restroom

Place at least 4 layers of toilet paper on top of the seat before using it. Wash your hands when finished.

Grimy Sink in Public Restroom

Pull the lever on the towel dispenser to lower a towel, then wash your hands. Rip off the dispensed towel and use it to shield your clean, wet hand while you pull the dispenser lever again and turn off the water faucet. Discard the towel. Tear off the second towel and use it to dry your hands. If no paper is available, use the ends of your shirt. Do not use the blow-dryer, which is a haven for germs.

No Toilet Paper in Public Stall

Call out to other occupants and seek their help in rolling or tossing paper to you from other stalls. Use disposable toilet-seat covers if available. If unavailable and there is no response from others, flush the toilet, partially open the stall door, and peer out. Move quickly to next stall to seek paper, or dash to the paper-towel dispenser, grab towels, and return to the stall.

Suspicious Buffet

Take food only from freshly filled containers. If you have doubts about how long the food has been sitting, wait until you see an attendant bring out a fresh tray. Avoid foods from the ends of the buffet, where the sneeze guard does not offer as much protection, or from below areas where the sneeze guard is soiled. Avoid raw seafood and foods containing mayonnaise, which are often food poisoning culprits.

ILLNESS

Flu Epidemic

Remain indoors, away from other people. If you must go outside, wear an N95 surgical mask and rubber gloves. Avoid areas where large numbers of people congregate, including movie theaters, dorms, barracks, shopping malls, and large office buildings. Do not use public restrooms. Do not share towels, even with family members. Empty wastebaskets and wash hands frequently.

Smallpox Outbreak

Follow instructions from public-health officials. Individuals with the virus will be placed in quarantine, but avoid coming into contact with others to be as safe as possible. If you think you have been exposed, stay away from family members and contact the local public-health authority. Victims in the "rash stage" of the virus (usually about 17 days after exposure) are the most contagious.

Tourette's Episode

Ignore the behavior (shouting, repeating words, coughing, throat clearing) until the episode passes. In rare instances, the victim may hit himself or others, bang his head, or display other dangerous behavior. In these cases, move the victim to a safe location, or remove all hard objects from the immediate area.

COMMON COLD

Rest. Drink plenty of fluids. Gargle with warm salt water for scratchy throat. Chicken soup may help fight infection through intake of salt, heat, and fluid. Zinc interferes with cold-virus replication in lab settings—zinc nasal sprays may reduce symptoms if used at first sign of cold. There is no clear evidence of colds being prevented or eased by echinacea or vitamin C, or being caused by overheating or chills.

Treat the victim with a doctor-prescribed antibiotic until the fever subsides and there is marked evidence of improvement, usually 5 to 10 days after initiating treatment. Symptoms include fever, nausea, vomiting, muscle pain, lack of appetite, and severe headache. Later symptoms include rash, abdominal pain, joint pain, and diarrhea. The disease is only transmitted through the bite of an infected tick and is not contagious between humans.

Seizure

Remove furniture and other hard objects near the victim to protect her from injury. Do not attempt to restrain the victim or force a hard object into her mouth, or you may cause additional injury. Do not attempt CPR or mouth-to-mouth resuscitation during the seizure. If the victim vomits, turn her onto her side to prevent asphyxiation.

Seasonal Affective Disorder (SAD)

Expose yourself to a greater amount of indoor light, leave window shades up and blinds open, spend more time outdoors when the sun is shining, and take a vacation to a sunny locale. Symptoms of seasonal affective disorder include fatigue, sadness, sleep difficulty, increased appetite, carbohydrate craving, irritability, weight gain, lack of energy, anxiety, and problems concentrating during winter months.

Obsessive-Compulsive Disorder (OCD)

Begin behavioral therapy immediately upon recognition of symptoms. Early indicators of OCD include frequent and excessive hand washing, repeatedly checking the locks on doors, repeatedly counting to the same number, and arranging objects in a precise order. Treatment for OCD typically includes frequent exposure to the objects provoking the obsessive-compulsive behavior.

Agoraphobia Attack

Call a close friend or relative to accompany you outdoors. Relax, then imagine yourself opening the door, leaving the house, and walking outside. Concentrate on breathing and staying relaxed as you conquer each step in turn.

INJURIES

Tooth Knocked Out/Broken

Pick up the tooth or piece of tooth by the crown (top), not the root. Rinse it under cool water, then place it back in its socket. If the tooth is broken or otherwise will not stay in place, put it in your mouth, between your cheek and gum to keep the root moist and protect the tooth from bacteria. Alternatively, place the tooth in the mouth of another person or in a glass of milk. Seek emergency dental care immediately. Do not transport the tooth dry or in water.

Broken Nose

Keep your head back and nose elevated to reduce blood flow to the injury site. Apply an ice compress to the nose to reduce swelling. Take ibuprofen or acetaminophen for pain.

Dislocated Jaw

Support the jaw to prevent further injury, either by holding the lower jaw in your hands or by placing a bandage under the jaw bone and tying it on top of the head. The bandage should be tight enough to hold the jaw in place, but not so tight that it cannot be removed quickly. Get to an emergency room as quickly as possible.

Cut/Severely Bitten Tongue

Rinse your mouth with a solution of one part hydrogen peroxide to one part water. Do not swallow the solution. Apply pressure to the tongue with a cold, clean, wet wash-cloth until the bleeding stops, then apply a towel-wrapped ice pack for 15 minutes. Small punctures will heal on their own, though severe lacerations may require professional treatment, including antibiotics to prevent infection.

Bleeding Gums

If the bleeding is an isolated incident, there may be a piece of food caught between the tooth and the gum. Floss to remove the item, then brush your teeth. Tie a knot in the floss to help dislodge a particularly stubborn object. Repeated or continual bleeding should be considered a serious medical problem and treated by a professional. Bleeding gums are generally due to infection of the gums and/or the bones supporting the teeth.

Split Lip

Apply pressure to the injury site with a cold, clean, wet washcloth until the bleeding stops. If the cut is deep and bleeding continues, seek emergency medical treatment. Avoid touching the laceration with food items to prevent pain and possible infection.

BLACK EYE

Sit down. Tilt your head back. Place a cold can of soda on your cheek (not your eye) for 5 minutes. Remove for about 10 minutes, then repeat until the swelling subsides. Other than the chill, there is no benefit from putting a steak on a black eye.

CONCUSSION

Try to talk about the incident that caused the concussion. If you are unable to remember the event, the concussion may be serious. Treatment options vary based on the severity of the concussion. Immediate symptoms of serious concussions include amnesia, confusion, headache, loss of consciousness, nausea, and vomiting. However, symptoms may not be present, may be difficult to spot, or may have a delayed onset. Do not engage in any vigorous activity until you have been evaluated by a professional.

CRACKED RIB

Place 5 strips of medical/athletic tape along the rib, spaced 1 inch apart, from the middle of the chest to the spine. Position 1 strip directly across the injured rib, 2 above, and 2 below. Immobilize the arm on the injured side in a snug sling to reduce pain and prevent the rib from shifting. Do not bend over, twist your body, or take deep breaths. Take an over-the-counter pain medication for discomfort, and seek medical attention. A single cracked rib that is not displaced will heal in several weeks.

DISLOCATED SHOULDER

Immobilize the arm immediately to avoid extreme pain at the shoulder and to prevent further complications, including tendon, ligament, and nerve damage. The ball of the humerus must be put back into the joint socket, a procedure that should only be performed by a qualified medical professional to avoid further damage to the arm and shoulder. Seek emergency care immediately.

TORN LIGAMENT

Sit down. Elevate the problem area above the heart, if possible, and apply an ice pack in intervals of 20 minutes on, 30 minutes off. Keep weight off the injured appendage, and seek medical attention. Longer-term treatment depends on the severity of the tear and its location. Generally, a partial tear will require immobilization of the injury, usually with a split or cast, for a few weeks to several months to allow the ligament to heal. More serious tears generally require surgery.

SPRAINED ANKLE

Take all weight off the ankle. Elevate the ankle above the heart, and apply an ice pack in intervals of 20 minutes on, 30 minutes off, to reduce swelling and pain. Immobilize the injury by wrapping it with a bandage in a figure-eight pattern, up and over the ankle and back around the foot. Seek medical attention to ensure that the ankle hasn't been broken or fractured.

BROKEN ARM

Immobilize the injury site with a splint extending to a joint above and below the break. Wrap the fracture in soft material (cloth, cotton, moss). Bind with firm material (branches, poles, boards, magazines) and tie with shoelaces to secure.

For fractures below the elbow, make a sling by securely tying together the sleeves of a buttoned-up shirt or jacket and slipping it over your head and around the back of your neck. Tuck the injured arm in the bulk of the jacket.

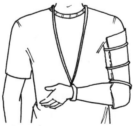

For fractures above the elbow, make a sling by running string or shoelaces around the back of your neck and tying them to the wrist of the injured arm. Place a pad of soft cloth material into the armpit.

AILMENTS

Boil

Apply warm-water heat to the boil with a wet washcloth or a hot water bottle, and take a hot shower twice a day. After the heat treatment, rub zinc oxide cream onto the boil to help bring it to a head. Do not pop a boil. When the boil has formed a head, cover it with gauze and allow it to drain on its own. After drainage, treat the area with a topical antibiotic to prevent infection, then dress it with sterile gauze. Large boils require treatment from a physician.

Stye

Put a moist, hot compress on the stye for 15 minutes, 3 to 4 times a day, to bring it to a head. The stye, which is the result of an infection of an eyelash follicle, must burst and drain of its own accord. If you touch the stye, wash your hands with soap and water to prevent the infection from spreading. Styes typically disappear within 5 days; see a doctor for a more persistent infection.

Tooth Infection

Treat discomfort with an over-the-counter pain reliever until you can get professional dental help. Infection of the pulp of the tooth requires either root canal surgery or tooth extraction.

Sensitive Tooth

Use a soft-bristle toothbrush, and do not use tartar-control toothpaste. Seek dental care for continual, painful sensitivity, which is caused by exposed dentin in the tooth. A cavity or gum disease may be the culprit.

Cold Sore

Apply rubbing alcohol every 3 hours to dry the sore area and reduce the visible blister. Place a cold compress on the site to reduce swelling. Wash your hands thoroughly after touching the cold sore to prevent transmission.

Swallowed Bling

If you must retrieve bling, stay close to home or another area with a convenient, clean restroom. Exercise, and drink at least 8 ounces of water once an hour to help speed digestion. Eat meals normally. The human body generally digests and passes food completely within 24 hours.

Heartburn

Neutralize stomach acids with an over-the-counter anti-heartburn medication. To reduce future occurrences, eat smaller meals, eat more slowly, and avoid citrus, onions, peppers, tomatoes, high-fat and spicy foods, alcohol, coffee, and carbonated drinks. Persistent heartburn should be treated by a doctor.

VOMITING

Do not eat solid food for 12 to 24 hours. To avoid dehydration, drink small amounts of water, about 1 ounce at a time. Gradually reintroduce a small amount of clear liquid every hour, such as chicken broth, apple juice, lemon-lime soda, or ginger ale, to restore electrolyte balance. Do not attempt to eat solid food until you have not vomited for at least 12 hours, then try bland, easy-to-digest foods like bananas, rice (white only), applesauce, and dry toast. If vomiting returns, limit your intake to clear liquids and try again after more time passes. Avoid dairy products, including cheese and ice cream, for several days after the sickness subsides.

LOST APPETITE

Make a ginger tea. Mix together the following ingredients: 1 teaspoon grated fresh ginger or ¹/₂ teaspoon powdered ginger; 2 cups hot water; ¹/₄ teaspoon peppermint leaf; ¹/₄ teaspoon anise seed; and ¹/₄ teaspoon cinnamon.

GROWLING STOMACH

Try to burp in order to release trapped gas that may be contributing to the stomach noises. Keep your mouth closed. Snacking on something—especially carbohydrates—may help relieve symptoms, as will taking antacids. Eating mints or chewing gum will aggravate the situation by releasing more stomach acid.

Abdominal Cramp

Drink chamomile tea, or take a single dose of activated charcoal slurry, according to the product directions. Avoid solid foods until the cramping subsides.

Diarrhea

Drink water (not milk) and avoid fatty and greasy foods. Take a prescription or over-the-counter antidiarrhea medication containing loperamide, unless the diarrhea is due to food poisoning. Offer children the BRAT diet: Bananas, Rice, Applesauce, and Toast.

Constipation

Eat one of the following foods to relieve constipation: cabbage, papaya (fresh or dried), prunes, coconut (fresh), asparagus, or soy products.

Nausea

Drink 2 cups of freshly brewed ginger tea. Stir 1 teaspoon grated fresh or $\frac{1}{2}$ teaspoon powdered ginger into 2 cups of boiling water. Ginger ales are not as effective as tea, as many do not contain natural ginger.

Morning Sickness

Eat 7 small, bland meals each day. Keep salted crackers on hand for snacking, and take 10 mg per day of vitamin B_6.

Caffeine Overload

Caffeine cannot be eliminated from the bloodstream except naturally, over time, generally in 3 to 4 hours. To speed absorption and processing, eat a full meal containing fresh fruit and vegetables, and drink several glasses of water. Symptoms of excessive caffeine consumption include headache, twitching, irritability, and irregular heartbeat.

Low Blood Sugar

Eat 1 tablespoon of honey immediately. Honey contains 15 grams of "quick" carbohydrates that will raise blood sugar in 15 to 20 minutes.

Hives/Rash

Administer over-the-counter diphenhydramine as quickly as possible, then every 6 hours for 1 to 2 days. Do not wait for the rash to develop fully before treatment. Hives are caused by the body's release of histamines; they may come and go for several weeks, though typical outbreaks last hours to days.

Dizziness

Change positions slowly from a prone or seated position. Avoid jerky movements of the head. Take aspirin to increase blood flow to the base of the brain. Most causes of dizziness are not serious, though it may indicate arrhythmia, heart attack, stroke, or shock.

INSOMNIA

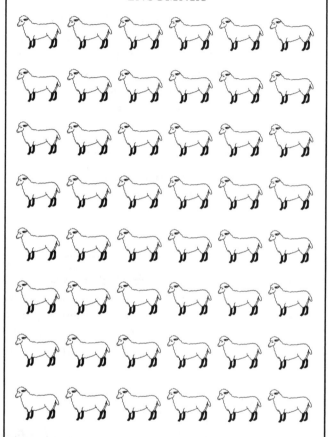

Take a warm bath; eat a bedtime snack; drink warm milk or herbal tea; cover illuminated clocks; lie on your back; rub your stomach; flex your toes. To prevent insomnia, avoid caffeine, nicotine, and alcohol. Light exercise or stretching an hour before bed can help relax muscle tension. Count sheep.

Look in a mirror and refamiliarize yourself with your appearance, age, and gender. Check your wallet for photographic ID to connect your face with a name, and look for indication of your home address. If you are at home—if your name appears on paperwork or prescription bottles within the house—stay there. Dial numbers preprogrammed in a mobile phone or found in a personal phone book, explain your situation, ask who the respondent is and if they can help. If you believe that you can find your way back, go outside and locate a newspaper box or vendor and read that day's newspaper to recover the date, the city and country you live in, and other circumstances of the day. Spontaneous temporary global amnesia—complete memory loss—is most common in middle-aged or elderly people and generally lasts less than 24 hours.

Migraine Headache

Consume a small amount of caffeine. Move to a quiet, dark room free of strong odors and lie down with a pillow supporting your head and neck. Place a cold compress on your forehead. Take nonprescription pain medication if available. Note: migraine triggers include alcohol, too much or too little sleep, stress, bright light, smoking, too much or too little caffeine, exercise, odors, birth control pills, skipping meals, MSG, nitrates, and menstrual cycles.

Ringing in Ears

Place 1 teaspoon of rosemary or lemon oil in a vaporizer. Sit in a closed room with the vaporizer running for 1 hour. Vitamin A and C supplements may also be effective treatment for tinnitus not caused by disease, hearing loss, or wax buildup.

Earache

Take an over-the-counter decongestant or ear wax softener if the earache is not accompanied by fever and/or hearing loss. Gently press under each ear, then massage just under the edge of the jawbone to relieve pressure in the Eustachian tubes. See a doctor for treatment of earaches accompanied by fever, as a prescription antibiotic may be required to fight the infection.

Eye Twitch

Close eye. Massage lid. Reduce caffeine intake, and get some rest. Eye twitching is most often caused by fatigue and is generally harmless.

Sinus Infection

Take an over-the-counter decongestant, in pill or spray form. Use a humidifier to keep nasal passages moist, but do not allow rooms to exceed 50 percent humidity or you will encourage mold growth and dust mites.

HICCUPS

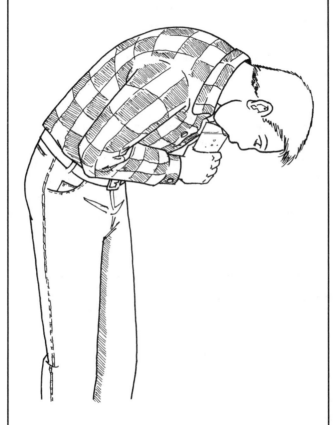

Fill a tall glass with water. Holding the glass in front of you, lean forward over the glass so that your mouth is on the rim farthest away from you. Tilt the glass so that the bottom moves toward you and the top away from you; drink the water as it moves toward the front of the glass.

HAY FEVER

Remain indoors on windy days, especially if there has been little rain. Avoid touching or rubbing your face or eyes. Take an over-the-counter allergy medication with anti-histimine and a decongestant, in either pill or spray form.

DRY MOUTH

Chew the rind of a lemon or lime. Increase humidity in your home with a humidifier or vaporizer, especially at night. Avoid mouthwash that contains alcohol or perox-ide, salty foods, dry foods, and foods and drinks with high sugar content, high acid content (fruit juices), alcohol, or caffeine. These ingredients will further dry out your mouth.

CHARLEY HORSE

Knead along the length of the muscle to increase blood flow in the area. Do not massage across the muscle. Stretch, drink water to rehydrate, and eat a banana to increase your potassium levels.

HEART PALPITATIONS

Breathe deeply and exhale slowly. Reduce caffeine con-sumption. Yoga and meditation may also be effective.

FIRST AID

Spurting Artery

Fashion a loop from string, rope, or a belt. Place the loop above the wound, then tie it off. Place a stick inside the loop. Twist the stick to tighten the loop just enough that the bleeding stops or slows. Tie the free end of the stick to the body to prevent it from coming loose. Use of a tourniquet of this kind may result in loss of the injured limb and should be considered only as a last resort, and only to prevent death from blood loss.

Choking, Self

Stand facing a waist-high blunt object (back of a chair or table, tree stump, ledge). Bend over so the object touches your body 6 inches above your waist. Drop forward hard and fast, forcing the air out of your abdomen and up your windpipe. Repeat until the item is dislodged.

Choking, Adult/Child

Perform the Heimlich maneuver. Stand behind the victim, wrap your arms around the victim's waist, and make a fist. Place the thumb side of your fist against the victim's upper abdomen, below the ribcage and above the navel. Grasp your fist with your other hand and press into her upper abdomen with a quick upward thrust. Do not squeeze the ribcage. Repeat until the stuck object is expelled.

Choking, Infant

Perform the infant Heimlich maneuver. Lay the baby down, face up, on a firm surface, and kneel or stand at his feet; or hold the infant on your lap facing away from you. Place the middle and index fingers of both your hands below his rib cage and above his navel, and press into the infant's upper abdomen with a quick upward thrust. Do not squeeze the rib cage. Be very gentle. Repeat until the object is expelled. Holding the baby facedown and slapping his back may not dislodge the stuck object and should be considered only as a last resort.

Choking, Pregnant Woman

Perform the Heimlich maneuver for adults as indicated on page 37, with this exception: Place your hands above the victim's belly, across the chest, instead of at the abdomen. This method is also effective for extremely obese victims.

Severe Burn

Stop, drop, and roll to extinguish open flame, or cover the burning area with a blanket to smother. Place the burn under cool running water to remove foreign material, cool the skin, reduce pain, and limit swelling. Remove clothing unless it is stuck to the burn. Cover with a clean, sterile dressing or a clean T-shirt; do not use a towel or other material with loose fibers. Call for help. Elevate a burned extremity to reduce swelling.

Chemical Burn

Irrigate the burn area with cool running water for 10 minutes. Meanwhile, gently remove the contaminated clothing. Try to limit additional exposure to the chemical agent. Cover the burn area loosely with a sterile cloth or T-shirt; do not use a towel or other material with loose fibers. Do not remove any fibers stuck to the burn. Bandage. Seek emergency medical treatment as soon as possible.

Heart Attack, Self

Chew one 325-milligram aspirin. Alert someone near you that you are having a heart attack and tell him to call for help. Stop all activity, lie down, and elevate your legs. Breathe, then cough, every 3 seconds until help arrives.

Heart Attack, Someone Else

Call for help, then begin CPR immediately.
1. Locate the lower tip of the breastbone, measure two finger widths toward the head and place the heel of one hand in this location, with your other hand on top of the first hand.
2. Lean forward so your shoulders are over your hands.
3. Compress. Push down on the chest, using the weight of your upper body for strength. Perform 30 fast compressions in 20 seconds.
4. Breathe. Blow two slow breaths into the victim's mouth.
5. Compress and breathe. Perform the compression-and-breath cycle until help arrives.

Lay the victim on her back. Elevate the feet 6 to 10 inches, maintain an open airway, and control any obvious bleeding. Wrap the victim in a blanket to maintain body temperature. Call for help. Do not give the victim anything to eat or drink.

Fainting

Place the victim flat on his back on the ground. Elevate the victim's legs and feet 12 inches to increase blood flow to the heart and brain. The victim should recover in less than 1 minute. Do not administer ammonia or other smelling salt–like treatments.

CHAPTER 2

BEAUTY & FITNESS

HAIR

Singed by Barbecue

Cut the hair above the singe line. Wash and condition to remove the burnt odor.

Bad Dye Job

Re-dye the hair, going darker rather than lighter. Using the ten-level system to classify hair color (1 is black, 3 is darker brown, 5 is medium brown, 7 is dark blond, and 10 is very light blond), choose a new dye color that is no more than two levels above the existing color.

Frizz on a Humid Day

Towel-dry your hair. Apply a small amount of olive oil or styling gel that contains oil to the palm of your hand and brush the product through your hair using your fingers. Do not use a brush or blow-dryer.

Hat Head

Wet the hair thoroughly, then restyle using hairspray or styling gel. Women with long hair can avoid hat head by pinning a small bit of hair near the crown into a bun before putting on the hat, then letting it free after removing the hat, so the hair on top will be full of body.

BIRD CAUGHT IN HAIR

Shield your eyes and face with your arm. With your other hand, grab the bird's feet and legs from behind, pull it from your hair, and toss the bird lightly away from you. Do not attempt to grab the head or beak.

Toupee/Wig Falls Off

Retrieve the wig. Inspect and remove any debris from the hair if the wig touched the ground. Stand in front of a mirror, plate-glass window, or metal reflective surface. Reapply the wig or toupee tape, use other available tape curled on itself to adhere to the wig and your head, or just place the wig directly on your head. Realign the ear tabs and press the wire "stays" slightly in at your temples. Check your hair positioning in a reflective surface and secure with bobby pins or paper clips, if available. Elastic in off-the-shelf wigs will stretch and weaken after 3 to 4 months of daily use; it, or the wig, should be replaced to ensure a snug fit.

Smoke Smell

Spray a strong perfume into the air above your head, then walk in a slow circle while the scent settles on your hair.

Gum in Hair

Place several ice cubes in a plastic bag. Hold the affected hair away from the scalp and apply the ice bag to the gum for 15 to 30 minutes, or until it is frozen solid. Hold the stuck section of hair between the gum and the scalp, then break the frozen gum into pieces. Gently pull the gum pieces from the hair with your other hand. If the warmth of your hand thaws the gum, refreeze and repeat until all the gum has been removed.

Shampoo in Eyes

Turn the shower taps to cold and flush your eyes. If shampoo remains, rinse your eyes with saline drops or eye-safe contact lens solution. Wear a plastic sun visor when washing hair for extra protection.

Bird Droppings in Hair

Comb or brush the droppings from the hair, then wash the hair or rub the spot where the dropping landed with a cotton ball soaked with rubbing alcohol. Hold your breath while removing the dropping and wash your hands thoroughly after removal to avoid a potentially fatal infection from the *Cryptococcus* fungus found in some bird droppings.

MAKEUP

Mascara Running

Hold a cotton ball under each eye to catch the running mascara. Close your eyes and use two more cotton balls to remove any remaining traces of the mascara from the eyelashes.

Applying Lipstick without Mirror

Open your mouth. Using your dominant hand, position the tip of the lipstick in the center of the bow of your top lip, with one of the fingers of your other hand positioned above it as a guide. Draw a half heart from the tip of the bow, then trace the top of your lip out to the edge of your mouth, using your guiding fingertip to keep the makeup steady. Repeat on the opposite side of the top lip. Place the lipstick at center of your bottom lip and trace to the corner of your mouth. Repeat on the other side. Do not rub your lips together or color will smear outside of your lips.

Stains on Clothing

Apply heavy-duty liquid detergent directly on the stain, allow to soak for 30 minutes, then machine wash with hot water. For whites, add ½ cup chlorine bleach to the machine, using the automatic bleach dispenser if your machine is equipped with one.

SKIN

BAD BOTOX INJECTION

Get an additional injection in the lateral fibers of the forehead to counteract inadvertently sad (fallen brow) or quizzical (brow pulled upward) expressions. Reaction symptoms include weakness, nausea, fatigue, flu-like reactions, and rashes, most of which will pass without treatment within several days. Remain upright for 3 to 4 hours following injections to help reduce complications from the toxin spreading to muscle tissue not intended to receive it.

TOO MUCH COLLAGEN

Fill a plastic bag with ice, wrap the bag with a thin cloth, and hold it at the injection site to reduce excessive puffiness and swelling. Leave in place for 10 to 15 minutes, then remove. Do not apply ice directly to skin. Bruising and dots at the injection site will disappear without treatment in about a week.

FROSTBITE

Thaw frozen digits in lukewarm—not hot—water only if there is no chance of refreezing, which can cause severe tissue damage. Apply sterile dressing to the affected areas. If available, take over-the-counter pain medication to treat the burning sensation that accompanies thawing. Do not rub frostbitten skin directly or rub with snow. Avoid applying direct heat.

WRINKLES

To prevent wrinkles in
forehead and around eyes

To strengthen mouth muscles
and prevent laugh lines

To mold chin and prevent
wrinkles around mouth

To relieve tension created by
previous exercise

Repeat this sequence of facial expressions for 5 minutes twice daily
to help prevent wrinkles.

Streaky Self-Tan

Scrub problem areas with a washcloth soaked in rubbing alcohol. Apply a layer of moisturizing lotion to counteract drying of skin from alcohol, then reapply the tanner.

Uneven Tan Lines

Dust the skin with a powdered bronzer, using a large makeup brush for even application.

Razor Burn

Apply hydrocortisone cream to treat irritation, but not more than twice a week or you risk thinning the skin. Avoid aftershaves and colognes that contain alcohol, which will dry the skin. To prevent razor burn, do not shave for at least 20 minutes after waking up to allow fluids that swell the surface of the skin while you're asleep to disperse; your skin will tighten, exposing more of the hair and allowing a better shave. Wet your hair for several minutes to soften it before shaving.

FACE

PIMPLE

Apply a warm compress to the pimple for 15 minutes. Remove, then place fingers on either side of the pimple and gently pull away. The pimple should expel its contents. If the pimple is not ready to pop, cover it with a dab of green-tinted makeup to conceal the blemish and counteract the redness.

BAGS UNDER EYES

Steep 2 bags of black tea in warm water for 2 minutes, then soak in ice water to cool. Squeeze out excess liquid. Place a tea bag over each eye for 15 minutes. The tannic acid in the tea will reduce the swelling.

STUCK IN ONE EXPRESSION

Massage the facial muscles regularly. Apply moist heat or take nonprescription pain medication to relieve pain; practice relaxation techniques; and increase your intake of B vitamins. If paralysis or weakness interferes with normal eyelid function and blinking, keep the eye moist with artificial tears or eye ointments and cover with an eye patch. Bell's Palsy is a form of temporary facial paralysis caused by swelling of facial nerves, the exact causes of which are unknown, but which can be associated with head trauma or viral infection. Symptoms generally begin to subside in about 2 weeks.

Extra Chin

Wear scarves, ascots, or loose-fitting turtlenecks to disguise excess fat around the neck. Avoid shirts with tight, button collars. Wear collared shirts without a tie.

Blotchy from Crying

Apply a cool washcloth to the face to reduce swelling and redness. Both symptoms are generated by the increased blood flow and muscular effort of crying, two physiological nervous system responses to emotional distress. Lie down and take deep, calming breaths.

Chapped Lips

Apply beeswax or petroleum jelly. Wear lipstick or sunscreen. Drink lots of water, especially during winter months. Do not lick your lips, which may make them feel temporarily moist but covers them with irritating salivary fluid. Rub your index finger at the side of your nose and rub oils onto your lips if no other balm is available.

Shaving Cut

Dip a cotton swab in rubbing alcohol and dab it on the cut, or apply styptic pencil or powder. Both substances are astringents that cause the contraction of blood vessels. Alternatively, place small pieces of toilet paper on the cut to encourage coagulation. When bleeding stops, wet the paper thoroughly, then carefully peel it off the cut.

EYES

Foreign Object in Eye

Flush the eye with cool running water or saline solution to remove debris. If you are unable to remove the debris yourself, ask someone to wash their hands thoroughly, then use their fingers to remove the object from the white of the eye. Avoid touching the pupil, cornea, or iris. Seek medical attention if the object cannot be easily removed.

Bloodshot Eyes

Close your eyes. Place a cool washcloth over each eye for 15 minutes to reduce redness.

Lost Contact Lens

Rely on your good eye until you are able to replace the lens. Keep one eye closed, or wear an eye patch. For a less conspicuous solution, use a thick black marker to color the inside of the lens on a pair of sunglasses on the same side as the missing contact.

Contact Lens Slides behind Eye

Close the eye. Massage the lid until the lens moves back onto the cornea, or lubricate the eye with drops until the lens slides forward. The eye is a closed "pocket" and a lens cannot get lost or stuck behind the eyeball.

LOST GLASSES

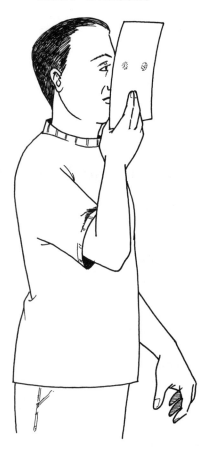

Draw 2 circles about the size of a pair of lenses on a piece of paper or cardboard. Use a pin or the tip of a sharp knife to poke at least a dozen small holes inside the circles. Hold the paper to your face and look through the holes.

HANDS

Broken Nail

File the nail to smooth ragged edges, then cover with an acrylic nail of the same length as your natural nails. If the cuticle is torn or bleeding, treat it with vitamin E oil before applying the fake nail.

Hangnail

Soak the finger in warm water for 15 minutes to soften the nail, then cut the hangnail with cuticle scissors or a nail clipper. Do not chew or tear at the hangnail or you risk injury and infection.

Broken Finger

Wrap a bag of frozen vegetables in a thin cloth, then place on the injured finger. Elevate the finger above the level of the heart to reduce swelling. If you cannot get to a doctor within several days, place the injured and one adjacent finger on a Popsicle stick or other flat, straight piece of wood and tape the fingers together and to the splint. Try to move the hand as little as possible.

Disguise Missing Finger

Insert a small piece of flexible tubing into the finger of a glove where the missing finger would be and wear regularly. Wear mittens in cold weather.

Fidgety Hands

Hold and squeeze a small rubber ball to keep fidgety hand occupied. Alternatively, hold a beverage.

Splinter

Sterilize a pair of pointed tweezers and a safety pin using rubbing alcohol. Grasp the exposed portion of the splinter with tweezers and pull to remove. If the splinter is buried, use a pin point to carefully scrape away several layers of skin until an end of the splinter is exposed, then grasp and remove with tweezers. Treat the wound area with topical antibacterial cream, then bandage. For children, numb the area with an ice pack before removal.

FEET

Plantar Wart

Apply an over-the-counter salicylic acid treatment and cover the wart with fabric adhesive tape. Leave the tape in place until it begins to fall off. Remove the tape and scrape off as much of the white (dead) tissue from the wart as you can. Repeat. If little progress has been made after several weeks, seek a doctor's help.

Athlete's Foot

Soak your feet in a solution of warm water and 1 tablespoon of tea tree oil 3 times per day until the condition disappears. Wear absorbent socks made from natural fibers, and change immediately if the socks become damp. Remove shoe insoles and allow them to dry overnight, and dust the insides of shoes with talcum powder.

Bunion

Wear shoes with ample room for toe movement. Choose shoes with flexible soles, heels less than 2 inches high, and about ½ inch of space between your longest toe and the tip of the shoe. Avoid high-heeled, narrow, or pointed-toe shoes. Go barefoot as much as possible. To treat pain from bunions, elevate your feet so they are higher than your heart and apply ice to the joint for 10-minute intervals several times an hour.

BLISTER

Sterilize a needle by dipping it in rubbing alcohol or holding it over a match for several seconds, until red hot. Holding the needle parallel to the skin, puncture the blister at its edge. Apply gentle pressure to squeeze out the fluid, then cover the blister completely with a bandage.

BRUISED FEET

Pad your shoes with shock-absorbing insoles. Stay off your feet as much as possible to allow the fat pads of the heels to heal and keep them from being further pushed from their place cushioning the heel bone. If your sneakers are old and their padding is compressed, replace them.

BODY

Cellulite

Maintain a normal weight, and reduce your weight gradually if you are overweight. Exercise regularly (particularly resistance programs like yoga and Pilates), and reduce your consumption of alcohol, caffeine, and highly processed foods. Eat fresh fruits and vegetables, and drink plenty of water. Though there is no nonsurgical cure for cellulite, there is some evidence that the herb gota kola and aloe vera cream can reduce symptoms.

Sore Muscles

Apply ice packs to painful areas for 20 minutes each hour. Stretch the sore muscle areas thoroughly to reduce the lactic acid buildup that causes pain and increase blood flow and oxygen in sore areas. Drink at least 64 ounces of water daily, and take ibuprofen for severe localized pain.

Too Thin

Wear fitted clothing to give your physique shape and good lines; double-breasted jackets add bulk. Avoid pinstripes, which give the appearance of length, and tight-fitting pants, which will only accentuate thin legs. Pleated pants will add the illusion of girth, but baggy pants will seem billowy and should be avoided. Dressing in layers can add appearance of bulk. Wear flats, not heels.

SADDLEBAGS

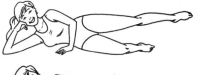

Lift.

Extend.

front-to-back hip swing

Leg down.

Leg up.

side leg raise

Perform exercises to firm the hips and outer thighs: the front-to-back hip swing and the side leg raise. Perform two sets of 12 to 15 reps on each side, 2 or 3 times a week, with a rest day in between.

Too Fat

Draw attention to your face with a bright necktie or scarf. Wear loose but not oversize clothing, and use contrasting colors (dark shirt with lighter jacket) to provide a slim appearance. Avoid horizontal stripes, double-breasted jackets, and pants with pleats or elastic waistbands. For women, wear pants that cover your shoe tops to give your body a longer appearance. For men, wear suit jackets with side or double vents to avoid accentuating a large rear end.

Forgot Deodorant

Wash armpits with water and hand soap, then rinse and pat dry with paper towels. If soap is not available, place 2 mint teabags in hot water, dip in ice water to cool, wring out, then place one under each arm for 2 minutes. A wet sprig of thyme rubbed under the arms will provide temporary odor protection.

Excessive Perspiration

Apply antiperspirant containing 12 percent aluminum chloride to armpits, palms, feet, face, back, chest, or other problem areas. Wear loose-fitting, light-colored cotton clothing to help mask visible sweat marks.

DIETING

Relapse Binge

Forgive yourself and start over. Binging is common for dieters. Look at it as a temporary setback rather than complete failure. Gather any snacks left over from your binge; give them to others or throw them away. Replenish your refrigerator and cabinets with healthful food choices, and resume your diet.

Chocolate Cake

Do not take a bite: Remember, the first bite is the beginning of a serving. Avoid defeatist thinking ("I'll never get thin anyway, so I might as well eat the cake"). However, dieting is not about deprivation, so eat a healthful dessert like fruit or nonfat yogurt in place of the cake. If you cannot avoid temptation, leave the table before the cake is served and return when everyone is finished eating.

The Munchies

Eat 5 to 6 small meals per day rather than 3 large ones—large meals tend to lead to a drop in blood sugar 3 to 4 hours after consumption, prompting snacking.

GUILT-FREE FOODS

unsalted pretzels

unbuttered popcorn

broccoli

rice cakes

mushrooms

bell peppers

cucumbers

water

Consume these foods without guilt.

Adjust your caloric intake to maintain your weight rather than lose it. Eat breakfast and snack during the day instead of "saving" your calories for a big dinner. If the food is served buffet style, walk the line without a plate and survey the offerings, deciding in advance what you will choose rather than just loading up as you go. Avoid alcohol. Plan a polite excuse or be ready to leave the room to avoid offerings of high-calorie foods you may feel socially obligated to eat.

THE GYM

SMELLY GYM SHOES

Place a fresh dryer sheet in each shoe. Place each shoe in a sealable freezer bag overnight. The shoes should smell fresh in the morning.

OVERBEARING TRAINER

Feign dry heaves to prove to the trainer that you've pushed yourself to your physical limit. Weakness and shortness of breath may also be effective in getting the trainer to lower his expectations, but these ploys could backfire and result in ever more strenuous attempts to toughen you up.

TRAPPED UNDER BARBELL

Yell "Spot! Spot!" to get the attention of others who can lift the barbell off of you. If you can move, carefully slide your body so the weight is supported by your hands above your chest, rather than over your head, neck, or abdomen.

DUMBBELL DROPPED ON TOES

Remove the dumbbell from your foot, then carefully remove your shoe and sock. If moving one or more of your toes causes sharp pain, it may be broken; sit down immediately to take weight off the leg. Ice the toe(s) for 15 minutes, then surround with cotton balls and tape to an adjacent toe. Walk slowly and carefully.

Sprint a step faster and lunge for the "kill switch" or yank the red power "key" from its socket on the control panel. If you cannot reach the control panel, keep pace as best you can and call for help.

FEELING DIZZY ON MACHINE

Stop the machine and your workout immediately. If you are lying down, avoid sitting up too quickly, which may exacerbate lightheadedness. Breathe deeply and exhale slowly until the dizziness passes, then drink a cup of cool water.

LOST IN STEAM ROOM

Hold your hand out in front of you and walk until you touch a wall. Maintain contact with the wall and follow it around the room until you reach the door. Call out to other occupants as you move to avoid collision. Alternatively, wait a few moments for the steam level to disperse and quickly exit before more is introduced. Steam is created either by pouring water on heated rocks or channeled in through vents. If you are wearing glasses, remove them.

AVOIDING GERMS ON MACHINE

Cover machine surfaces with fresh clean towels before touching. Hold folded-over paper towels in each hand before grabbing the machine's handle/bar, or wear gloves. Use a fresh set of towels for each machine. Do not touch your face with your hands until you have washed them thoroughly with soap and water after your workout.

JOGGING

Heat Exhaustion

Stop jogging. Get out of the heat immediately. Rest in a shady place, and drink plenty of water or a sports drink. Wait at least 30 minutes before moving, or until the dizziness, weakness, headache, and rapid heartbeat subside.

Muscle Cramps

Massage and stretch to increase blood flow to the cramping muscle. Rehydrate yourself with water or a sports drink. Apply an ice pack to relax tense muscles. Later, if you still have pain or tenderness, use a warm towel or heating pad or take a hot bath.

Shin Splints

Use the R.I.C.E. treatment method: REST the legs by avoiding jogging; apply ICE to the shins for 15 minutes several times each day; COMPRESS the shins with a bandage to reduce swelling; and ELEVATE the legs above the head.

Lost

Retrace your steps, or ask a passerby for directions. If you are in a remote wilderness area, stick to a marked or well-traveled trail—or follow a road—until you reach a populated area.

CHASED BY PACK OF DOGS

Enter a car or nearby building as quickly as possible. Some breeds will tire after a short chase, while others may continue to chase you over long distances. Climb a tree only if you are able to get more than 4 feet off the ground.

Foot in Pothole

Put your weight on the good leg and use a stout tree branch as a temporary crutch. If available, use a bandage to bind the ankle tightly to compress swelling and limit foot movement.

Knee Gives Out

Sit down immediately to take weight off the knee. When immediate pain subsides, return home, walking at a slow pace, placing little weight on the knee. Place an ice pack on the knee for 10 minutes 3 or 4 times a day for several days, then apply heat treatments (ointments, soaks, heating pads) for several days. Take ibuprofen to reduce inflammation. Wear a knee brace or elastic bandage. Do not climb stairs unless necessary. A doctor may prescribe a cortisone injection and is likely to recommend strength training for the quadriceps.

TATTOOS

Infection

Have the tattoo examined by a doctor right away. A tattoo infection should be considered a serious medical emergency—it may be minor, or it could be something as serious as hepatitis or HIV. To reduce the risk of infection, make sure the tattoo parlor appears clean, sterilizes all equipment, has sinks with hot water and soap in the bathrooms as well as the studio, and that the staff wears latex gloves. If the shop uses disposable needles, ask the tattoo artist to remove the needles from sealed, sterile packaging while you watch.

Pain While Being Tattooed

Choose a fleshy area with some muscle tone—such as a bicep or the back of a calf—where tattooing is less painful. Avoid tattooing areas where skin is close to the bone, such as the wrists or ankles, knees, or along the spine or skull. Choose a simple tattoo that's mostly outline, with very little fill. Do not take pain medications or drink alcohol before the tattooing procedure to avoid thinning the blood, which can cause excessive bleeding and potentially alter the look of the tattoo. Wear headphones, chew gum, or bite a pencil to manage pain, or decide to enjoy it.

DISGUISE EX'S NAME
WITH NEW TATTOO

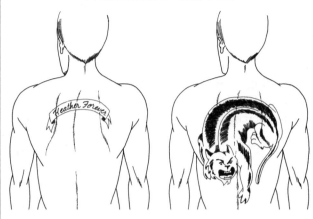

Cover with a more elaborate tattoo in darker ink. Incorporate some of the lines of the original tattoo.

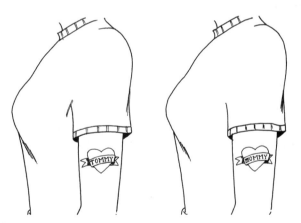

Alter the name to express more enduring sentiments.

PIERCINGS

Leave jewelry in place to avoid premature closing of the piercing, which may trap the infection. Keep the area dry and free of potential irritants like hair or clothing. Treat the piercing daily with rubbing alcohol and a topical antibiotic (for body piercings) or an antiseptic mouthwash (for oral piercings). Infection may require treatment with antibiotics, so seek medical attention if it exhibits swelling, yellow pus, heat at the piercing site, or inflammation. White discharge from a piercing is normal during healing and is not a sign of infection.

HOLE HEALS

Have the piercing redone. Leave jewelry in the hole until the wound heals completely. Depending on the body part, this can take anywhere from 4 weeks to 6 months.

HIDE FROM PARENTS

Wear clothing that effectively covers the area. For ear piercings, wear your hair long. For eyebrow piercings, wear large sunglasses with thick plastic frames. For a tongue piercing, speak as little as possible.

CHAPTER 3
HOME

WALLS

Paint Spill

Scrape the spill area with a spoon or a piece of stiff cardboard to remove as much of the paint as possible. For acrylic paints, soak the area with clean, cold water, then blot with a clean cloth. Repeat until paint is removed. For oil-based paints, remove by blotting with mineral spirits.

Hole in Drywall

Cut the ragged edges of the hole with a matte knife to make a square or rectangular opening. Measure and cut a piece of replacement drywall and fit it into the opening. Affix painter's tape or gauze over the seams on all four sides of the replacement panel, then cover with a thin layer of spackle. Allow to dry. Sand smooth and paint.

Loose Shelf or Fixture

Remove the shelf from the wall. Insert appropriate-sized drywall spreaders or masonry/brick anchors, depending on the wall surface material, into the existing holes. Re-attach the shelf by screwing support screws through the spreaders/anchors fully until they open behind the drywall or spread and grab the masonry/brick.

CROOKED ARTWORK

Place a level on top of the frame. Grasp the frame securely at both sides and shift the painting left to raise the right corner and right to raise the left corner, until the artwork is level. If artwork is hung on a nail or hook without the use of picture wire, remove the artwork from the wall and add a second nail to the left or right at the same level as the existing nail. Rehang the artwork.

BLEEDING WALLS

Call an exorcist. Wear a cross around your neck. If blood is seeping, don work gloves and wipe affected area with rags soaked in a solution of 1 part holy water to 4 parts tap water. Sprinkle stained areas with holy water. If blood is gushing or beds begin to levitate, vacate the house and do not reenter until the priest arrives.

FLOORS

Loose Tile

Remove the existing grout with a file, then regrout tiles smaller than 4 inches square. For larger tiles, file down the existing grout, pry up the tile, remove the adhesive and grout from the tile, and readhere the tile to the mesh backing on the floor using a commercial tile mastic. Regrout.

Flood Damage

Remove all furniture and small appliances from the home as soon as it is safe to do so. Allow them to air dry thoroughly and have them checked by a trained technician before using. Have the home's electrical and plumbing systems checked before using them. Clean floors, walls, and cabinets using an all-purpose detergent and hot water. Sanitize with a solution of 2 tablespoons of chlorine bleach mixed with 1 quart of cold water. The home should be inspected for mold by a professional home inspector or insurance adjuster as soon as possible.

Creaky Floorboard

Pour powdered soap or talcum powder into the cracks around the creaking board. Tamp into cracks with the edge of a piece of stiff cardboard. Test and repeat until the squeak disappears. For older flooring boards attached with visible nails, remove nails and replace with nails slightly larger in diameter.

FALL THROUGH FLOOR

Spread your arms wide to distribute your weight across unbroken flooring. Place your palms down and push your body up and back, away from the hole. If you are in the hole up to your waist or farther, lean forward onto your forearms and push to raise as much of your body mass as possible above the hole. Repeat until free. Do not grasp at furniture legs above the hole or kick with your legs below.

STAINS ON CARPET

RED WINE	**Blot wine with an absorbent cloth.** Saturate the stain with club soda or cold water, blotting until no more wine transfers to the cloth. If the stain remains, apply a paste of borax or baking soda and water (at a ratio of 3 to 1). Smear paste onto stain with an old toothbrush and let dry. Vacuum, then repeat until no more stain can be removed.
BLEACH	**Sponge the stain immediately with cold water** to remove as much acid as possible. Mix baking soda and water to make a paste (at a ratio of 3 to 1) and rub onto the stain. Scrub into carpet with an old toothbrush, then let dry. Vacuum, then repeat until no more stain can be removed.
GREASE, MOTOR OIL	**Use a dull knife or spoon to remove as much as possible.** Blot remaining liquid with an absorbent cloth. Work shaving cream into the carpet with an old toothbrush. Wipe it off with a damp cloth, then sponge with cold water. If the stain remains, apply dry-cleaning fluid (be careful not to wet the carpet backing with it), then sponge the stain with a damp cloth.
BLOOD	**Use a dull knife or spoon to remove as much as possible.** Blot remaining liquid with an absorbent cloth. Sponge the stain with a sudsy mixture of liquid laundry enzyme detergent and cold water, then sponge with cold, clean water. If the stain remains, sponge with a mild bleach such as lemon juice or hydrogen peroxide (do not let it saturate the carpet), then sponge with cold clean water. Repeat as needed.

PLUMBING

Flooded Basement

Remove water less than 1 inch deep with a wet vacuum. For deeper water, pump out using a commercial pump. Use a rotating floor fan to dry the area. Replace all wiring if the water has reached outlet level. Have all basement-level mechanical systems (furnace/boiler, hot-water heater) checked by trained professionals before using.

Frozen Pipe

Turn on the water at each tap, one at a time, to isolate the frozen pipe. The water will not run out of the tap connected to the frozen section. Once you have located the frozen pipe, turn off the water supply where it enters the property to reduce the risk of a flood if the pipe is cracked. Access the pipe and heat the frozen section with a hair dryer, then turn on the main water supply. When the frozen section is thawed, the water will begin to flow.

Burst Pipe

Immediately turn off the water where it enters the property. Turn on all taps until the pipes are empty. Locate the broken section. Cut out and remove the broken pipe section using a pipe cutter or hacksaw. File down burrs. Replace the section with a threaded slip-on coupling. Turn on the water and inspect the site to be sure fix holds.

Clogged Sink

Remove all dishes from the sink. Place a toilet plunger over the drain opening, pressing down to form a tight seal, and plunge several times. If the clog does not clear, feed the metal tape from a tape measure into the drain and push up and down to clear the clog. If the clog remains, don rubber gloves, place a bucket under the sink trap (the "J" shaped pipe under the sink), remove the trap using a plumber's wrench, clean out, and replace. Commercial drain cleaners may work, but their high sulfuric acid content can damage pipes.

Ring Lost Down Sink

Shut off water tap. Peer down the drain with a flashlight. If the ring is visible, retrieve it using the end of a wire hanger bent into the shape of a hook. If the ring is not visible, place a plastic bucket underneath the sink trap (the "J" shaped pipe under the sink) and remove the trap with a plumber's wrench. Wearing rubber gloves, empty the trap contents into the bucket and look for the ring. If the ring is not in the trap, it is not retrievable.

Septic Malfunction

Immediately stop using disposals, toilets, and washing machines. A washing machine alone may add 60 gallons per cycle to the septic tank. Have an expert check the drain field and the water level in the tank, then pump it out and repair as necessary.

Toilet Won't Stop Running

Turn off the water supply to the toilet; turn it back on before each use. To troubleshoot the problem, remove the toilet tank cover and, while the water is running, inspect the flapper to ensure it falls to completely cover the gasket to the toilet; it may be caught on the chain or have come off its mounting bracket. Press the flapper onto the gasket and hold. If the tank fills and the water stops running, the gasket is worn and should be replaced. If the toilet still runs, replace the entire fill mechanism.

Rat in Toilet

Close the toilet lid immediately and weight it down with a heavy object. Attach a straw to the end of a funnel, feed the end of the straw into the gap between the toilet seat and the bowl, and slowly pour ½ cup of chlorine bleach into the toilet through the funnel. Wait 15 minutes, or until you do not hear any movement in the bowl, then flush. The rat should be small enough to exit through the waste pipe the same way it entered.

Stuck in Toilet

Turn off the water supply to the toilet. Flush to empty the bowl. Spray dishwashing liquid into the toilet bowl around the stuck body part and pull to remove.

ENERGY SYSTEM

Blown Fuse

Inspect fuses for blackened glass to identify the blown fuse. Pull out or unscrew the blown fuse and replace it with a new, properly rated fuse. If you cannot locate the blown fuse by visual inspection, test each fuse by swapping in the new fuse.

Gas Smell

Open all doors and windows. Make sure the range and oven are off and that all pilot lights are lit. Even if you find the source of the problem, leave the house for several minutes to allow it to air out. If you are unable to fix the problem on your own by relighting a pilot light or turning off the oven or range, call the gas company to report the problem and remain outside the house.

Pet Electrocuted from Chewing Wires

Do not touch the animal. Turn off the power at the fuse box: Look for a switch marked "master" or "main" and move it to the "off" position. Using a wooden broom handle, separate the pet from the wiring. Feel for a pulse. Take the pet to an animal hospital immediately for treatment if it is still alive.

Broken Lightbulb in Socket

Cut a potato in half.

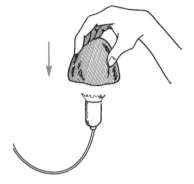

Shut off the power to the light, then place half of the potato over the broken bulb and firmly press down.

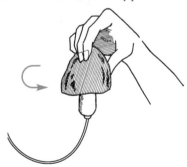

Turn the potato to remove the broken bulb.

Air Conditioning Blows Out in Hot Weather

Check the circuit breakers to determine if the breaker to the A/C system has been tripped—the system should be on a dedicated circuit. Move the breaker to the "on" position if it is off. If the system does not have a dedicated breaker, turn nonessential appliances off, then restart the system. If the system does not turn on, open the windows, move to the lowest floor of the house, and keep your feet in a pot of cool water.

Heating Goes Out in Cold Weather

Check the pilot light if the system is a gas-fired boiler; if the light is out, relight. If the pilot will not light, make sure gas is entering the home by testing the range-top burners in the kitchen. If the burners light, the house has gas; call for repair. If the boiler is working but the house is cold, bleed air out of the pipes by opening the bleeder valve on the radiator on the top floor. For oil and electric heat, call for repair. Wear sweaters, hats, mittens, and scarves as necessary.

FURNITURE

Broken Chair Leg

Nail an upside-down toilet plunger to the seat to replace the detached leg. You may need to saw it to the appropriate height. Turn down nail points if they are sticking through the seat. Alternatively, remove remaining chair legs and place the seat atop an overturned bucket. Sit carefully.

Creaky Mattress

Turn the mattress over and test for creak. If the creak remains, rotate the mattress so that the head of the mattress is at the foot of the bed. Test. If the creak persists, place a phone book or small flat block of wood under the mattress at the creaking location to compress the springs and reduce noise.

Leaky Water Bed

Flatten a large cardboard box. Slide the cardboard under the mattress. Lay atop the mattress for several minutes, then check the cardboard for damp areas to indicate the locations of leaks—generally at the mattress seams or corners. Patch the holes using a dinghy- or bicycle tube–repair kit. Do not use the mattress for several hours to allow the patch to set.

Caught in Sofa Bed

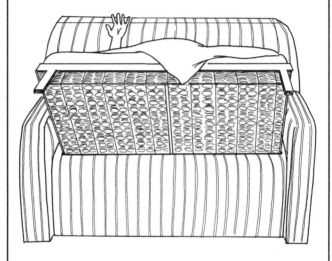

Grasp the top edge of the bed if your arms are free and pull your lower body away from the folding section. If your arms are pinned, dig your heels into the mattress and push to lift the folding section enough to shift position. Wriggle to the edge of the bed, grasp a sofa arm, and pull yourself free.

WINDOWS

Painted Shut

Insert the blade of a putty or matte knife between the window and the sill sides. Move the blade along the edges to cut through the excess paint. Repeat on the other side of the window if it has been painted on both sides. Push the window firmly but carefully outward, then upward to open. If the window is still stuck, gently tap the upper edge of the window frame with a rubber mallet to loosen.

Body Part Stuck through Broken Window

Place a vase, pillow, or thick blanket around the body part, then pull it out of the window. Do not break the remaining glass in order to avoid flying glass shards and further injury.

Curtains Catch Fire

Open the window, tear the curtains off their support rod, and throw them outside, provided it is safe to do so. If you cannot open the window, or if the burning material may cause injury or additional fires outside, extinguish the fire with a bucket of water or with a household extinguisher.

EXTERIOR

CLOGGED GUTTER

Remove leaves and other debris from the gutter with a rake, broom, or gloved hands. Place plastic leaf traps over all unsealed downspout openings and cover all horizontal rain gutters with chicken wire to prevent future clogs.

LEAKY ROOF

Cover holes with sheets of plywood. Cover the plywood patches with a plastic tarp or a layer of thick plastic sheeting. Place strips of wood along each edge of plastic and nail in place, using one nail every 18 inches. Use as few nails as possible to avoid adding more holes to the roof than necessary. Seal cracked joints around protruding air vents and fans with plastic roofing compound.

LOCKED OUT

Check for rear or side windows that may be unlocked. Press palms flat against the glass at the sides of the window frame and push upward. Alternatively, insert any available thin, sturdy implement into the base of the window and attempt to pry it open. If you must break a window for entry, break the smallest window possible that is still large enough to crawl through. Reach through the broken pane and open the window—do not crawl through broken pane.

FALL INTO EMPTY POOL

Lie still. Carefully test the movement of your arms and legs to ensure nothing is broken, and that movement is possible; leaf litter may have broken your fall. Sit up slowly, especially if you are dizzy or feel faint. Walk or crawl to the shallow end of the pool and climb out. If you cannot get to the shallow end, use a cell phone to call for help, or yell until a neighbor hears you.

NOSY NEIGHBOR

Construct a wooden fence at least 6 feet high, with no more than ¼ inch between pickets.

YARD

DEER EATING PLANTS IN GARDEN

Place coyote urine capsules around the perimeter of the garden, spaced no more than 10 feet apart. Coyotes are natural deer predators, and the scent of their urine is an effective deterrent. Avoid spilling urine on plants and flowers. Replace the capsules every few weeks, or as soon as the odor fades.

RABBITS EATING PLANTS IN GARDEN

Grind dried red chile peppers to a fine powder using a mortar and pestle. Sprinkle the powder along seeded rows of plants and vegetables and around the bases of existing plants. Reapply chile powder after heavy rains or watering. Wash all vegetables before consuming.

SQUIRREL STEALING BIRD FOOD

Drill a hole in the bottom of a very smooth metal salad bowl. Run the wire of the bird feeder through the hole so the bowl hangs directly above the feeder, upside down, and rehang the feeder. The bowl will prevent squirrels from climbing down the wire to the feeder. Make sure the feeder is far enough from the ground and other objects that the squirrel cannot leap to it from the sides or below.

Inoperable Sprinkler Head

Turn the water off. Turn the radius adjustment screw on the sprinkler head to the full "on" position. Remove the sprinkler nozzle and wipe away any visible dirt. Remove the screen under the nozzle and clean it. Turn the water on to flush all hoses, turn it off, replace the screen and nozzle, then turn the water back on.

Raccoons in Trash

Place refuse in metal trash cans. Secure the can lids with bungee cords. Rinse trash cans with ammonia once a week and sprinkle red pepper dust on and around the receptacles.

Poison Ivy

Rinse the affected areas with warm running water to remove as much of the urushiol oil as possible and reduce spreading of the rash. After several minutes, increase the water temperature until it is as hot as you can stand it, being careful not to burn yourself. The hot water releases histamines from the skin, providing temporary relief. Treat the rash with hot or cold packs, or cortisone cream, to relieve itching. Avoid using soap or scratching or rubbing the affected area, all of which may spread the oil and hence the rash.

Put on protective gear. Layer clothing to include a long-sleeve shirt and zipped jacket, two pairs of long pants (jeans under sweat pants) tucked into two pairs of socks, leather shoes or boots, thick work gloves, and an insect veil. Spray the nest with a commercial aerosol containing pyrethrin and rotenone to paralyze the insects. When wasps are not flying from the nest, dislodge it from the house with a rake handle or dig it up from the ground (making sure to get all larvae). Burn the nest on a grill, or place it in a large sealable freezer bag and freeze overnight, then dispose.

TREE FALLS ON HOUSE

Inspect the inside of the roof from the attic or top floor. If the tree has damaged plywood or rafters, call a professional roofer. If there is no visible damage, the attic is dry, and the roof is not pitched, put on shoes with rubber soles and go to the roof. Working from above the tree, never below, use shears to cut off smaller branches and a bow saw to cut the trunk into smaller pieces. Remove the wood. Never use a chain saw on a ladder.

GARAGE

Box Avalanche

Duck and cover your head with your arms and curl into a ball on the floor. If a shelf has fallen toward you, stay as close to the shelf/wall as possible to avoid being hit by objects falling out as well as down.

Box Stuck in Rafters

Set an extension ladder under the rafter, climb up, and hand the box down to someone below if it is full of heavy materials. If the box is light and the contents aren't fragile, place a mattress on the floor and knock the box down with a telescoping lightbulb changer or two brooms held together with duct tape.

Bats Living in Garage

Turn on a bright light and leave it on all night, several nights in a row. The bats will leave of their own accord.

Carbon Monoxide Buildup

Do not enter the garage. Open the garage door with a remote opener to vent the gas. If the garage must be opened manually, open the door from the outside. Open any side doors if it is possible to do so without entering the garage. Wait 10 to 15 minutes, enter the garage, and turn off the car engine.

STUCK UNDER CAR

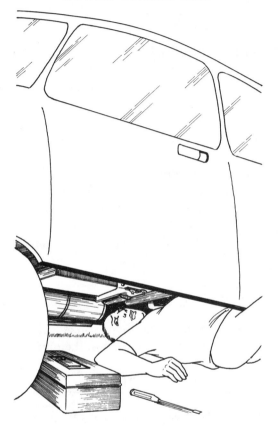

Suck in your gut, grasp the edge of the undercarriage of the car, and pull to drag yourself free. If you cannot hold in your gut for the length of extrication, suck in and pull or push toward the edge of car in small stages until free.

Garage Door Closes on Car

Stop the car immediately to limit damage. For a manual garage door, pull up on the handle and move the door to its fully open position. Electric garage door openers manufactured after 1993 should—if they haven't malfunctioned—have sensors that prevent the door from closing on a person or object and will automatically reverse the door to its fully open position when it strikes something.

Missing Tool

Think back to the last time you had visual or physical contact with the tool. Revisit the locations of major or minor tasks that may have involved the tool. If you believe the tool has been borrowed but not returned, confront potential suspects, including your children, spouse, relatives, and neighbors. If the suspect denies having possession of the tool, conduct an independent search of the suspect's room, car, home, yard, or garage. If the search is unsuccessful, ask to borrow, or simply borrow, a tool or item of equal value.

INTRUDERS

BURGLAR

Call the police immediately. Give your exact location if you are calling from a mobile phone. Leave the house if you can do so without confronting the intruder. If you cannot get out of the house, stay where you are and lock the door. Alert the burglar that the police are on their way and wait for help to arrive.

COCKROACHES

Eliminate all traces of excess moisture—roaches can go weeks without food but will die in less than a week without liquid. Stuff steel wool into the space around pipes to limit movement. Sprinkle powdered boric acid around cracks and crevices under the kitchen sink, but keep it away from areas where food is prepared and out of the reach of children or pets.

GUEST WHO OVERSTAYS WELCOME

Declare a household emergency such as fumigation, severe mold remediation, or asbestos removal that requires all occupants to evacuate immediately. Alternatively, tell the guest you are going to paint their room and must remove all the furniture. Do not pretend to be leaving on vacation—the guest may offer to housesit in your absence.

BIRD IN HOUSE

Use a broom to gently maneuver the bird into a room with a window and a door. Open the window, leave the room, and close the door. Wait for the bird to fly out. This method also works for stray squirrels.

Mice

Fill holes around pipes with steel wool to prevent mice from moving around the house freely, seal any holes in walls or to the outdoors, then humanely trap or kill using traps or commercial bait/poisons.

Squirrels

Locate the entry point, generally around eaves and down-spouts or where branches come into contact with a structure. Seal the hole with close-knit steel mesh and roofing compound or metal flashing. Squirrels may find a new hole, necessitating professional trapping.

Termites

Move all untreated wood away from basement floors, walls, and window sills, which are all areas where termites enter structures. Termites should be controlled by commercial poison, applied by an exterminator.

Mold

Eliminate all sources of moisture, which mold requires to grow. Once affected areas are dry, scrub using household detergent and water and allow to dry completely; wear rubber gloves and an N95 respirator mask during cleaning. Seal with a commercial waterproofing agent. Mold in heating or ventilating systems or in areas covering more than 10 square feet requires professional treatment.

CHAPTER 4
PETS

DOGS

Runaway

Instruct someone to remain at home in case the dog returns. Check the closest neighboring yards and areas that may be familiar to the dog from walks, then expand the area of search methodically to cover a ten-block radius and all nearby parks. Call the dog's name or whistle while conducting the search. Instruct the person at home to print "Dog Missing" flyers, including the dog's name, description, and photograph; your name and telephone number; and "reward" (do not specify an amount). Post flyers in the area if the search is unsuccessful. Supply all nearby animal shelters with the dog's description.

Poop on Shoe

Remove your shoe and seal it in a plastic zipper bag. Place the bag in the freezer for at least 3 hours. Remove the shoe from the freezer when the poop is frozen and chip it off with a flat-head screwdriver. Wash the screwdriver.

In Heat

Push the dog down immediately if the animal humps or mounts people or inanimate objects. Repeat as necessary and be consistent in discouraging this behavior. In many cases, mounting behavior is done to display dominance, though in some young dogs (male and female) it may be to relieve sexual frustration.

EMERGENCY RAIN GEAR

tail

paw → THANK YOU ← paw

HAVE A NICE
DAY

paw → ← paw

head

Cut or tear holes in a plastic shopping bag for the dog's paws and head. Use a kitchen- or yard-sized bag for larger breeds. Carefully slip the bag over the dog's head and ease the front and back paws through the holes.

← knot

Tie the bag handles behind the tail for added security.

Shedding

Wrap your hand with a long strip of masking tape, sticky-side out, to form a glove. Blot furniture using the front and back of the tape glove; discard and repeat. Also effective, if available: a lint brush or specially designed pet hair brush (available at pet stores), or a vacuum with an upholstery attachment. Brush the dog every day and dispose of hair to reduce the amount of shedding on furniture.

Barking During the Night

Bring the dog inside if it's yours; use earplugs if it isn't. Do not rile or further agitate the dog by yelling.

Dog Fight

Spray the dogs with a hose, dump a bucket of water on them, or use the straw end of a broom if no water is available. Avoid using your hands or you risk a bite.

Bites Visitor

Instruct the visitor to wash the bite with soap and warm water if the skin has been broken. Move the dog to another room and close the door. If the dog's rabies vaccination is up to date, the visitor should not require shots, but should monitor the wound for signs of infection. As the pet owner, you can be held liable for your dog's behavior, but a homeowner's insurance policy may cover you in the event of a bite.

Sprayed by Skunk

Mix a cleansing solution by combining 1 quart of 3 percent hydrogen peroxide, 1/3 cup baking soda, and 1 tablespoon liquid dish soap in a bucket. Place cotton balls in the dog's ears. Put on rubber gloves. Using a sponge, spread the solution evenly through the dog's coat, taking care to avoid getting it in the dog's eyes, nose, and mouth. Rinse with clean, cool water.

Rabies

Keep the dog away from humans and other animals and call animal control authorities immediately if you suspect rabies. You can contract rabies if saliva from the infected animal comes into contact with your eyes, nose, mouth, or an open wound. If instructed to take the dog to an animal hospital, protect your hands and arms with heavy gloves, long sleeves, and a sturdy jacket; place a muzzle on the dog's mouth; and crate it. Call your doctor if your dog is diagnosed with rabies.

Choking on Bone

Grasp the dog around the waist from the rear. Place your fist just behind the ribs and compress the dog's abdomen with 3 to 5 quick pushes. Repeat. Check the dog's mouth to ensure the bone has been completely removed. If you are unable to dislodge the bone, immediately take the dog to the nearest veterinary hospital.

Hold the dog's paw between your knees. Using tweezers or pliers, take hold of the thorn and pull gently but firmly. Inspect the paw to be sure the thorn is completely removed. Clean any cuts in cold water. Apply a bandage. Do not attempt to remove glass or a firmly embedded object—prevent the dog from walking on the injury and take it straight to the vet.

CATS

Up a Tree

Obtain a bath towel and a ladder. Set the ladder in a stable position at the base of the tree, climb, and approach the cat while calling and speaking to it in a soothing manner. Wrap the cat in the towel to prevent scratching and descend the ladder. If the cat is too high, call the fire department.

Clawing Furniture to Shreds

Cover furniture ends and edges with aluminum foil or wide masking tape to create surfaces not as pleasing to scratch, or treat furniture with a citrus-scented spray, an odor cats tend to avoid. Rub a scratching post with catnip and place it near the furniture the cat likes to scratch. Place the cat near the scratching post and use your own fingernails to scratch the post, cuing the cat to the proper behavior.

Bringing Kills into House

Pick up the kill using rubber gloves or a shovel and dispose of it in a tight-seal outdoor trash can without fuss or scolding, which may be misinterpreted as attention or praise. Put collar bells on the cat to reduce its hunting effectiveness, decreasing the number of kills and thus kills brought into the house.

LOST

Check the house thoroughly: Cats can squeeze into tiny spaces, and the cat may be stuck somewhere inside. Walk the neighborhood, loudly calling the cat's name. Post flyers with the name, description, and a photo of the cat; your name and phone number; and note of a "reward" without mentioning the amount. Bring a flashlight to see an injured cat that might be holed up in a dark place. If unsuccessful, call nearby shelters and animal hospitals.

DRINKS ANTIFREEZE

Look for signs of poisoning, including excessive thirst and urination, vomiting, and uncoordination. Bring the cat to a vet or animal hospital immediately—do not induce vomiting. If you can locate the antifreeze, rinse the spill area thoroughly with running water, then scrub with detergent and rinse again to remove all traces. Consumption of a single teaspoon of antifreeze can kill a cat.

BROKEN LEG

Pick up the cat. Gently move the leg into a more natural position, then tape or bandage the leg to a small piece of wood—such as a ruler—to create a splint and keep the leg immobile. Take the cat to a vet or animal hospital.

PERFORM THE HEIMLICH MANEUVER

Kneel and hold the cat in front of you, close to your chest. Place one forearm under the cat's front legs and hold him up and outstretched, facing away from you. Place the fist of your other hand just below the bottom rib. Give 2 or 3 quick, firm pushes inward to force the air out of the diaphragm and dislodge the object.

About to Give Birth

Make a "birthing box" in the final two weeks of the cat's pregnancy. Use a cardboard box large enough for the mother and her kittens to recline in. Cut a large opening so the mother can enter and exit, at least 4 inches up the wall so the kittens can't escape. Stack newspaper or towels in the box and place it in an out-of-the-way location. If possible, suspend an infrared heat lamp 3 feet above the box. In most cases, cats can give birth without human intervention. After the birth, the mother should cut the umbilical cords and tear open the kittens' membrane sacs; offer your assistance if she does not do so on her own.

Won't Use Litterbox

Clean the litter regularly, removing feces every 2 days and changing the litter once a week. If the cat still refuses to use the litter box, try changing the brand of kitty litter. Or, if you recently changed the brand, change it back.

Male Cat Sprays

Block the cat's view of other male cats outdoors; the sight of these "competitors" may be causing the spraying behavior, which the cat uses to mark his territory. Close doors in front of screens to eliminate the odors of other males. Place several litter boxes around the areas where the cat is spraying, and clean sprayed objects with an enzymatic cleaning product. Yelling or screaming at the cat may only encourage spraying.

Urine

Blot the stain with paper towels to remove as much of the urine as possible. Soak the area with white vinegar, then steam clean. If the odor persists, use a commercially available product created specifically for the purpose of removing urine odor.

Cat Allergies

Use an air purifier (preferably a commercial-sized unit) in the main living area, plus one in each bedroom. Vacuum regularly, making sure the vacuum filter is clean and the bag has plenty of room left. Brush the cat daily to remove loose dander. Bathe the cat once a month using a mild pet shampoo to remove proteins from cat saliva that may be an irritant.

Cat Scratch Disease

Check for a small bump or blister at the bite or scratch site, a low-grade fever, and swelling of the lymph nodes closest to the injury location. (An injury to the arm will cause the lymph nodes under the armpit to swell and become tender.) In most cases, symptoms will disappear without treatment in a few weeks—though lymph nodes may remain tender for months. See a doctor if you suspect cat scratch disease (caused by the *Bartonella henselae* bacterium), as antibiotics are sometimes necessary.

BIRDS

LOOSE IN THE HOUSE

Close the curtains and turn off all the lights. Birds will typically stay motionless in a dark room. Use a flashlight to locate the bird. Gently pick the bird up and return it to its cage.

LOOSE OUTSIDE THE HOUSE

Check all adjacent trees, bushes, and windowsills, whistling and calling the bird's name. Birds with clipped wings will not travel far, and caged birds tend to lose muscle mass and the capacity for skilled flight. Act quickly: Birds are targets for predators such as cats and hawks.

WON'T SHUT UP

Cover the bird's cage with a cloth and turn out all lights in the room. The bird should quiet down and fall asleep.

PARROT CURSES

Reinforce acceptable word usage with food treats or toys. Hold a cookie while you teach the parrot to say "cookie," or cover its cage while you say "good night." While it is impossible to "unteach" the bird, eventually it will use only those words it hears frequently. Never keep a parrot in your bedroom.

FISH

CRACKED AQUARIUM

Mark the ends of the crack with a grease pencil and take a photo, then check the crack each day. If the crack is not growing or leaking, leave it alone. If it is, transfer all tank contents to a new tank as soon as possible. Empty the cracked tank, dry it, then scrape away the area around the crack with a razor blade. Apply acetone to the crack area with a paper towel, allow to dry, then treat the crack with a nontoxic silicone sealer suitable for aquarium use. Allow to dry overnight, then refill.

DEAD FISH

Remove the dead fish with a fish net and discard (flush or bury). Clean the fish net with dish soap and rinse thoroughly. Place any remaining fish in a temporary holding tank or bowl and thoroughly clean the main tank with an aquarium-safe cleanser (available at pet stores) to minimize risk of transmission if the fish died of disease. Never clean aquarium glass with a household glass cleaner: Most contain ammonia, which is toxic to fish.

JUMPS OUT OF BOWL

Gently push the errant fish into a wet fish net—do not pick it up or you risk dropping the fish or damaging the gills. Return the fish to its bowl.

STUCK IN TANK DECORATION

Gently push the fish from the rear using a fish net until it is able to swim free of the obstruction. If fish is still stuck, hold the decoration just above the tank and push the fish gently out and back into the water using a wet net.

Fighting

Feed fish regularly. If fighting persists, separate fish into different tanks or partition the tank using a piece of glass. Fish fight due to overcrowding, being kept with too many of the same species, incompatibility (aggressive fish swimming with docile fish), or lack of food. Ensure the fish are compatible, have adequate space to roam, and are well fed.

Algae in Tank

Remove the tank from direct sunlight and do not light the tank more than 10 hours per day. Change the water, rinse the gravel, and clean the filter in the tank once a week to minimize nutrient growth. Green algae can be removed from tank glass by introducing an algae-eating fish such as the suckermouth catfish.

Cat Grabs Fish from Bowl

Scare the cat off—house cats will typically play with a catch before killing and eating it. If the fish is alive and appears to be uninjured, scoop it up with a wet fish net and return it to the tank. If it swims normally, leave it alone. If it appears to be injured and cannot swim, remove it from the tank, place it on a wet towel, and examine it for injury. Apply an antiseptic such as betadine to the injury site using a cotton swab, then return it to the tank. Do not keep the fish out of water for more than 1 minute.

Losing Scales

Remove any coral in the tank, as well as other objects with rough surfaces that may be causing the scales to rub off. Plecostomus catfish will occasionally eat the slime coating from some fish, causing scale damage. Remove the catfish to another tank, or partition the tank with a piece of glass to separate it from the other fish.

Freeze in Outdoor Pond

Make sure the water is at least 18 inches deep, and keep a hole in the ice to allow for gas exchange between water and air. Before the water freezes, reduce the fishes' metabolism and allow them to adjust to colder water by slowing the feeding schedule to once every few days, then once per week. After the thaw, resume feeding, but on a slow schedule as metabolism returns to normal, and until all ice has melted.

RODENTS

LOST IN THE HOUSE

Call the animal's name (if it knows it) or use a familiar squeaky toy to get its attention. Close all interior and exterior doors and search the house systematically, keeping doors closed and blocked with a towel under the doorframe even after searching a room to keep the animal contained. Check inside cabinets, under appliances, and in and under couches. Place a container with food, water, and a blanket or cloth the animal has used before just outside your front door, in case it manages to get outside. Consider setting a humane rodent trap to recapture your pet without injuring it. Crate other pets, especially cats and dogs, until the rodent has been located.

GNAWING AT CAGE

Move the animal to a glass cage, or use an empty aquarium. Alternatively, experiment with a larger mesh cage so the animal feels less confined. The mesh openings should be small enough that the animal's head cannot get caught.

BITTEN BY RAT

Clean the wound with soap and water, apply an antibiotic ointment, and dress the injury site. Get a tetanus booster if yours is not up to date, and monitor for symptoms of rat bite fever, including fever, chills, rash, sore throat, and aching in joints. See a doctor if symptoms develop.

FERRETS

LITTER TRAINING

Confine the ferret to its cage except when it is out for short periods of play. Ferrets are fastidious about hygiene and will avoid soiling their sleeping areas. Provide a litter box in the cage, as well as nesting material or a sleeping tube and food and water bowl. If you observe the ferret relieving itself, pick it up and place it in the litter box. If the ferret continues to soil the other areas of the cage, increase the size of the litter box to at least half the area of the cage until the ferret learns that it must use the litter or soil his sleeping/eating space.

DEHYDRATION

Administer a 1:1 solution of corn syrup and water, or honey and water. A ferret too sick to eat may be coaxed into drinking a 1:1 mixture of liquid nutritional formula and water. Ferrets have a fast digestive system, and should be hand-fed every 4 hours when sick or dehydrated.

INTESTINAL OBSTRUCTION

Administer 2 inches of cat hairball laxative paste—available at pet stores—every 8 hours for 1 day if you suspect the ferret has swallowed a foreign object but is acting and breathing normally. If the ferret is exhibiting signs of intestinal distress (difficulty breathing, vomiting, seizures), take it to an animal hospital immediately.

HERMIT CRABS

CANNIBALISM

Separate crabs of significant difference in size to deter cannibalism. An aggressive crab may attempt to remove a crab from its shell and inhabit the loser's shell itself. If you hear "chirping" and notice one crab in a position slightly above the opening of another crab's shell, remove the aggressor and isolate it from other crabs.

LEGS FALLING OFF (MOLTING)

Remove the crab from a shared habitat at the first sign of molting (missing limbs, clear gel-like new limbs, or a fishy odor) and place in an isolation tank with at least 6 inches of sand and several different sizes of empty shell. Molting crabs are vulnerable targets for other crabs when they shed and then regenerate their exoskeleton as they grow larger. Molting crabs prefer darkness, and will burrow deep into the sand or enter a large shell.

NAKED CRAB

Rinse the empty shell in water. Wash your hands. Pick up the crab and dip it in water to remove any debris. Using your index finger, gently curl, but do not force, the crab's abdomen into its shell. If the crab will not enter the shell, put it in an isolation tank with several shells of different sizes, including a new one the same size as the old one, and let it choose a new home.

Remove all sand substrate from the tank and discard.
Disinfect all crabitat toys by placing them in boiling
water. Rinse the tank with warm water, then use paper
towels to crush and kill any remaining mites, paying special attention to the corners, then rinse. Bathe the crab by
placing it upside down in warm water. When it comes out
of its shell, wet it thoroughly, then let it dry in another
container before placing it back in its shell.

SNAKES/REPTILES

LOST IN AIR DUCTS

Turn off heating/cooling system. Position a fan at a vent and blow cool room air into the duct. Position a hair dryer at a duct in another location and blow warm air into that duct. The snake should move away from the direction of the cool air and seek the warmed air. Be ready to grab the snake when it approaches the hair dryer.

SALMONELLA

Stay hydrated. Salmonella generally passes without treatment in 5 to 7 days. Wash your hands with soap and warm water thoroughly after handling the snake or any objects in its cage. The snake is more likely to harbor the bacteria in its intestine without displaying symptoms than to become sick.

HYPOTHERMIA

Place a heating pad at a low setting in the snake's cage. Fold a medium-size hand towel over the pad, then put your hand on the towel. If you cannot leave your hand in place for several minutes, the heating pad is too hot; turn it down and try again. Once the heat level is correct, place the snake on the towel.

DEPRESSION

Increase the size of the cage so the snake can stretch out. Introduce objects that the snake can use as vertical climbing aids. Add a larger water container in which the snake can immerse itself, and make sure the cage is warm enough (80° to 85°F during the day, 70° to 75°F at night). If the snake refuses to feed, try offering a live food item (or a dead one, if the snake has refused live prey).

TARANTULAS

BITES

Apply ice or a solution of meat tenderizer and water soaked into a cotton ball to the bite area. Tarantula bites are very weakly poisonous and generally do not induce a reaction.

KICKING HAIR

Remove the hairs using a tweezers if they penetrate the skin. Treat with a local antibiotic and an anti-itch cream. Tarantulas sometimes kick barbed hairs from their abdomens as a natural defense mechanism.

BROKEN LEG

Do not attempt to set or treat a broken leg. The tarantula will shed the leg at the next molt and replace it with a new one.

WON'T EAT

Use a heating lamp to ensure the cage is a constant 75° to 85°F. Make sure the water dish is full. A large tarantula can go weeks without eating before it molts, but it needs sufficient water to survive. Tarantulas that are not molting will sometimes not eat if they are too cool. Remove any leftover food bits from the cage to reduce the presence of mold.

CHAPTER 5

SPORTS & HOBBIES

FOOTBALL

TAKING A HARD HIT FROM A LINEBACKER

Position yourself low to the ground to present as small a target as possible. Relax as best you can as the hit comes. Lift your feet off the ground to avoid knee and ankle injuries. Land flat, letting the ground absorb some of the momentum, and exhale deeply. Then take a deep breath, jump back to your feet, and get yourself back to the huddle, showing no ill effects.

KICKING A FIELD GOAL IN A BLIZZARD

Clear the snow from the space around where you will be planting your foot and kicking the ball. Visualize the ball going through the uprights under perfect conditions, without any snow or wind. Keep the ball on a slightly lower trajectory than normal to reduce wind interference in flight, focus, and kick the ball with the clean purpose you would in practice.

PLAYING IN EXTREME HEAT

Hydrate every 10 minutes, drinking approximately 1 quart of water per hour. Apply sunscreen on any exposed skin to prevent sunburn, which traps heat in the skin. Do not drink more than 1½ quarts per hour, or you may induce hyponetremia (over-hydration); symptoms include fatigue, dizziness, and nausea. Avoid drinking alcohol for a full day prior to the game.

Pulled Hamstring

Ice down the entire affected area for 10-minute intervals and take over-the-counter anti-inflammatory medication. Do not return to play. Rest the muscle for a couple of days, then begin to gently stretch it out, stopping at the first sign of pain. Before working out, apply moist heat on the hamstring, and ice the muscle immediately following the workout. If it is not painful, you may run lightly with a shortened stride. Avoid sprinting until the injury is fully healed.

Concussion

Take yourself out of the game and back to the sidelines. Apply ice to the back of your neck to keep any swelling down. Get as much rest as possible, avoid overtaxing activities, and consult with your doctor. Do not drink any alcohol until your doctor has cleared you for normal activities again.

Forgot the Play

As a receiver, find an open spot on the field and wave your hands frantically to show the quarterback how open you are. If the play goes away from you, you have likely done no harm. If the pass comes your way, you will have made a brilliant ad-lib play, rather than having made a mistake.

Catching a Wet Football

Position yourself to catch the ball in the cradle of your arms, held close to your body rather than making a riskier reaching grasp for the ball. Don tactile receiving gloves if they are available.

Recovering Fumble in a Pile-up

Go fetal, surrounding the ball with as much of your body mass as possible, tucking in your arms, knees, and head. Close your eyes and stay clamped around the ball regardless of grabbing, wrenching, and elbowing at the bottom of the pile. Remain stationary until the ref completely unpiles the bodies. Stand and hold the ball aloft triumphantly.

BASKETBALL

Loose or Tight Rim

Shoot the ball with a high, soft arc, aiming for the front of a loose rim with a small amount of back spin—try for a swish or contact with the front of the rim to break some of the ball's momentum and nest it into the net. For a tight rim, drive the ball inside for closer shots, or bank a shot off the backboard to negate some of the rim's lack of bounce.

Shooting Winning Free Throw

Follow your normal shooting routine precisely, concentrating only on your motions and shutting out any other distraction. Take long, smooth breaths, inhaling through your nose, exhaling through your mouth. Picture the ball going cleanly through the net. As always, aim for the front of the rim.

Avoiding Being Posterized

Jump up as high as possible and slam your hands onto the forearms of the offensive player to keep from getting dunked over in a poster photograph–worthy manner. Focus on breaking her grip and control of the ball rather than getting hold of the ball itself. Outside of the basket, try to cut off her path to the hoop by standing at an angle to the rim.

SHATTERED/COLLAPSING BACKBOARD

Step past the end line behind the backboard—the structure will come forward if torn off its moorings. Bend toward the floor and cover the back of your head with your hands.

Winning a Jump Ball

Time your jump to go up exactly following the ball as it leaves the referee's fingers. If you are playing against a smaller player, wait for the ball to reach its full height from the ground before tapping it to a teammate. If you are playing against a taller opponent, back-tap the ball slightly before it reaches its apex.

Wearing Bobos

Play an efficient, hard-nosed, old-school game, keeping flashy passes and wild shots to a bare minimum. Be willing to take charges, play stiff D, and rebound like an animal. If you can sell yourself as a utility baller, you will still be given ample opportunity to play. You are better off wearing wack kicks and having a solid game than wearing top-of-the-line shoes and playing like a chump.

Taking a Hard Charge

Anticipate where your opponent will try to drive inside, beat him to that spot, and stand still. Cross your hands in front of your body, placing them squarely over your groin. Stand with your knees slightly bent, ready to roll backward at the first contact from the offensive player. When you fall backward, throw your arms out and in back of you to cushion the fall and exaggerate the force with which you were hit, to signify to the refs that a foul has been committed.

BASEBALL

POP-FLY FIELDING COLLISION

Go loose and roll backward on impact, keeping hold of the ball, if you have it, at all costs. Keep your concentration on the ball and be ready to make a play even if neither of you have been able to catch it. At the first sign of a pop fly, gauge your position and shout whether you'll be able to reach it, listening for shouts from other teammates. If you are called off, stop running and duck down and out of its path.

TEAM IS "CURSED"

Pack your squad with young players who don't know or feel less shackled by your club's tortured history. Invite the fans to take a more defiant and optimistic view of the situation. Hire a manager unfazed by superstition and bide your time.

HIT WITH FASTBALL

Twist your body to take the shot to the fleshy part of your upper arm or leg rather than on a bone in your hand or shoulder. Toss the bat aside and take your base. Show as little pain as possible, until you are back at the dugout. Apply ice to the bruised area.

Forgot Coach's Signals

Run aggressively for any opportunity you see to advance a base. If questioned, tell the manager that you thought you detected a flaw in the defense that you could exploit. If you are successful, there's no problem; if you fail, you can still claim to be doing all you can to win.

Bench-Clearing Fight

Tackle an opposing player on natural grass or infield dirt—stay off AstroTurf to avoid turf burn. Wrestle aimlessly until umpire takes control of the game.

Caught in Rundown

Scream at the opposing players as you run toward them to break their concentration. Stay on the baseline as you charge back and forth to avoid an automatic out. Hope for an error or an overthrow, or for a teammate running from another base to advance safely.

HOCKEY

Puck in the Stands

Duck and cover your head with your arms immediately if the shot goes awry. Keep your eyes on the puck at all times while it is on the ice.

Broken Stick during Game

Wave the broken stick end at your bench to alert your teammates of the situation, then drop the stick immediately: You are allowed to continue play as long as you do not keep hold of the broken stick. Skate directly to your bench and either grab a new stick if handed to you or, if play is intense, skate in to let another player dart onto the ice to replace you.

Fight

Grab your opponent's jersey and shoulder pads and yank them over his head. If you are both locked in, keep hold of your opponent's furthest arm (their likeliest punching arm) and keep your chin and nose tucked into your shoulder.

Absorbing a Check into Wall

Square your body to the wall to absorb the impact equally. Drop low to improve your leverage and push off the wall with both hands. Relax and stay loose when you are near the wall and be mentally prepared to take a hit at any time.

SOCCER

Soccer Hooligans in Stands

Hide or remove any clothing with clear team affiliation. Blend in with exclamations of noncommittal enthusiasm ("Yeah!" "Woooo!") and make your way slowly—to the bathroom if anyone asks—away from the rowdy section to safer ground from which to watch the match.

Evading a Slide Tackle

Maintain forward momentum and tap the ball slightly in the direction opposite and forward of the approach of the defending player's slide. Extend your stride to hop clear of the tackle, stepping forward to retrieve the ball, which will have also kept your momentum.

Blocking a Penalty Kick

Ignore the kicker and focus on the ball itself. With the ball only 13 yards away, you will not be able to react after the ball is kicked. Time your lunge for the moment the ball leaves the kicker's foot, making an educated guess based on the first split-second's motion as to which side of the net to jump for. Extend your body horizontally across the face of the goal with arms outstretched, covering as much space as possible. Remember: The expectation is for a goal to be scored; if you are able to block the kick, you have performed a minor miracle.

Confronting a Referee

Maintain a respectful tone and make your point as clear-cut and as unemotionally as you can. Do not touch, closely approach, or threaten the ref. If you are having difficulty with a particular player, gently point out to the referee that the player needs to be watched closely.

Making a Header

Move into the ball's line of flight. Bend your knees and arch your back. Tense your neck muscles and contact the ball with your forehead at a point directly over your eyebrows.

GOLF

Getting Out of a Sand Trap

Stand 30 degrees to the left of your target. Aim for the sand about 3 inches in front of your ball—to compensate for the cushioning effect of the sand—and swing with a slow, pendulum-like motion.

Pushing Ahead of a Slow Foursome

Line up a shot that sails directly over their heads. Apologize, saying that you were trying for the fairway, but that you forgot your glasses and are half-blind without them. Then ask to play through.

Ball Hits Bystander

Ascertain if an actual injury has occurred, apologize profusely, and offer to sign the ball for the bystander. Tell him it might be worth something someday—once you fix the hitch in your swing.

Releasing Frustration Without Throwing Club

Tense your entire body tightly into itself, clenching your fists, jaw, stomach, and shoulders for a count of ten. Then release, relax muscles, and exhale for a count of ten. Repeat as necessary.

Driving into a Headwind

Shorten your swing arc by widening your stance and choking down farther on your club to keep the ball low to the ground. Do not overhit—the resulting backspin will lift the ball higher into the wind.

Partner Inappropriately Dressed

Make your partner carry both bags. Appear as though you are consulting his advice, as you would a caddy, when in sight of club members. Have the partner "help" you line up angles and select your clubs. Be sure to tip him at the end of the round.

Sudden Thunderstorm

Listen for the thunder—by the time you hear it, lightning is likely only about 10 miles away. If stuck on the course, move to a point of low terrain away from trees, which can conduct electricity. If you feel your skin begin to tingle or hair stand on end, squat on the balls of your feet, place your hands over your ears, and lower your head to make yourself the smallest possible target should lightning strike. If you have a golf cart, get inside and sit out the storm. Do not touch the steering column or wheel.

TENNIS

Broken Racket

Play out the point with broken strings; you have no other option. As soon as the point is concluded, you may change your racket. If the breakage occurs during a first serve that is out, you may change your racket, but the server will get her first service to do over.

Court Has No Net

Affix a thin laundry line, string, or a combination of any available extension cords, shoelaces, jacket sleeves, or plastic shopping bags tied end to end to the court posts. Treat all balls that go under the rope as net points. If available, hang sheets, towels, or jackets over the line to form a wall. Alternatively, set a row of deck chairs along the net line and play over them.

Tennis Elbow

Stretch your forearm by extending your arm in front of you, bending your wrist down, and pulling your hanging fingers toward your chest with your other hand. If you can't give resistance without pain, you should stop playing and apply ice to the injured area for 10 minutes.

TREATING AN INJURED BALL BOY

Elevate twisted ankles or wrists. Apply consistent but gentle pressure until medical help arrives.

OVERCOMPETITIVE OPPONENT

Slow down. Use much more deliberate actions than usual at every turn to frustrate your opponent off his game. Take frequent water breaks. Check and recheck your racket strings. Ask your opponent friendly questions about his service and strokes.

RETURNING 110 MPH SERVE

Shorten the length of your return swing, keeping your follow-through to about 18 inches or so. Hit the ball as flat as you can, which will result in a faster return shot and turn incoming speed against the server.

SWIMMING

Swimmer's Ear

Carefully clean the ear canal and apply antibacterial eardrops or boric acid. In severe cases, you may put the drops on a small sponge and place the sponge in your ear canal to keep the medicine in place.

Green Hair

Wet your hair before swimming and work some conditioner into it. Slip on a tight swimming cap to keep your hair from coming in contact with the water, whose hard metals (copper and iron, for example) cause the color change. For already-green locks, use a chelating shampoo specially formulated for your condition.

Water Up Nose

Take a deep breath in through your mouth, then lower your head back under water and blow sharply through your nostrils. Raise your head above the water and repeat.

Swimsuit Lost in Turnaround

Calmly finish your lane and return. As you reapproach your suit, act surprised. This will demonstrate your dedication and intensity, which will stay with people longer than your direct embarrassment.

Swimmer in Other Lane Splashing

Time your lanes so that you go out when the offending party has reached the opposite side of the pool, allowing you to minimize your interaction. If the problem persists, pretend to have a coughing attack in her direction as you swim past.

Leg Cramp

Immediately flip over onto your back. Lift the cramping leg out of the water, rubbing it with one hand while your other hand works to stabilize your position. If you are out in a lake, begin paddling back to shore in this position, remaining face up.

Surviving a "Polar Bear" Swim

Work up your adrenaline by yelling and screaming loudly before plunging into the icy water. Bring an old blanket to sit on so your suit doesn't freeze to the ground. Wear aqua socks or something similar on your feet to avoid being cut by ice, and bring extra warm socks and layers of dry clothes for when you emerge from the water. Bring a thermos of a hot liquid to drink in case you get the chills.

CYCLING

Popped Bike Chain

Dismount and place just the top links of the chain on the smallest chain ring on your crank set. Raise the bike off the ground and turn the pedals forward until the chain catches back fully on the teeth of the chain ring, then adjust the gears so that you are in your original setting.

Lost Bike Lock Key

Cut four slits in the top of the barrel of a Bic pen and insert it into the cylindrical lock, turning clockwise, for an older U-lock. For newer locks and/or noncylindrical locks, use a pair of bolt cutters to snap the cable.

No Lights on Bike at Night

Strip down or don extra layers of clothing so that your lightest-colored garments are most visible. If you have a light-colored shirt or other garment, put it in a very visible place facing the cars behind you. If you happen to have or can locate aluminum foil, flatten it out and hang it from the back of your shorts or pants. Ride a route well-illuminated by streetlights. Sing loudly and make whooping noises.

Car-Doored

Throw your weight backward. Stand on the pedals and above the seat. Apply only the rear brakes. Turn slightly to the side to disperse the impact as you hit the door. If you land in the street, move immediately toward the curb to get out of the way of traffic.

No Bike Lane on Street

Ride in the street with the flow of traffic, at least 3 feet from parked cars. Watch for cars that have suddenly stopped in front of you or have just pulled in to park, as both are more likely to have doors open into your path. Maintain speeds only at which sudden and complete braking is possible. Always wear a helmet when riding.

Shoelace or Pants Tangled in Chain

Brake to stabilize the bike and regain your balance, leaning off the seat until your feet are on the ground. Pull your bike off the road. While grasping the chain as close to your front derailleur as possible, roll it backward slightly until the chain is untangled from your garments.

SKIING

COLLISION WITH ANOTHER SKIER

Wait until you come to a stop, lie still, and assess your injuries before moving. Wiggle your toes and fingers, hands and feet, arms and legs, making sure everything works before log-rolling back into a sitting position. Assess the condition of the other skier and take action as necessary.

STUCK ON LIFT

Zip up your coat, pull your hood down, bundle up, and sit close to your companion to share body heat. Do not attempt to jump off the lift even if it seems relatively close to the ground, or you risk injury from landing on unknown terrain or objects beneath the snow. Stay on the lift until it either goes back in motion or a rescuer arrives.

FROSTBITE

Get indoors and remove all wet clothing. Immerse the affected body parts in lukewarm water until the sensation gradually returns. Do not use hot water, as your skin will be numb to burning. Put on dry clothing layers and drink a warm beverage. Apply sterile dressing and warm compresses to the area, taking care not to rub against your skin.

Avalanche

Face down the mountain and use a freestyle swimming motion to stay atop the cascading snow as best you can. If you are buried, keep your arms and hands over your face to maintain a breathing space. Move your limbs and attempt to free your head of debris immediately after the avalanche stops coming and before the snow starts to pack down.

Skiing on One Ski

Hang your free leg over toward the remaining ski to keep your center of balance. Stay on your edges to control your speed and direction.

Snowblindness

Go indoors immediately. Rinse your eyes with cool, disinfected water. Apply cold compresses and cover your eyes for 24 hours. Cut small slits in gauze, place over your eyes, and cover with dark sunglasses to limit light entering your eyes if you cannot keep them completely covered.

Hypothermia

Warm yourself gradually by adding layers of breathable clothing such as wool and/or moisture-wicking fabrics. Increase your physical activity and take in warm liquids and high-sugar and carbohydrate foods. If you have a partner, utilize body-to-body contact to warm up. Avoid alcohol, caffeine, and tobacco, and wear only dry clothes.

FISHING

Outboard Motor Fails

Position the crankshaft so the points are closed, pry open the breaker arm, and insert a clean business card between the contacts. Let go of the breaker arm, allowing the points to grip the bottom of the card, then drag the card through the contacts, cleaning them of oil and grime.

Boat Springs Leak

Place a flat life preserver weighted from the top over the hole as a temporary plug. Bail water out of the boat using any cup or container. Return to shore immediately.

Waders Full of Water

Stay upright to prevent water weight from tipping you over. Use your pole vertically to help maintain balance. Once on shore, either unfasten and remove the waders to empty the water or lie down on an incline and let the water drain past your chest.

Outdo Buddy's Fish Tale

Allow the buddy to finish his story. Select a quantifiable detail you wish to top (number or size of fish caught, leaping ability, length of fight) and increase by 30 percent. For mythic overtones, increase all factors by 100 percent, adding inclement weather and equipment malfunction.

FISHHOOK IN FLESH

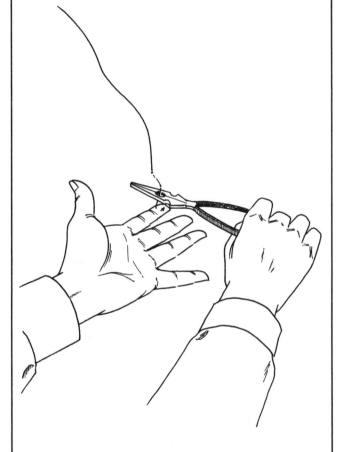

Clip off the end of the hook with a pair of needle-nose pliers. Pull the unbarbed end of the hook through the wound to remove. Apply antiseptic and dress the injury site.

SPELUNKING

HEADLAMP GOES OUT

Wait for as long as you are able to allow your eyes to adjust to the darkness (it can take as long as an hour for eyes to fully adjust from bright light to darkness). As you wait, visualize the features and path you have just traversed as far back as you can recall. Then retrace your steps carefully, moving slowly and with sure footing, using touch-contact with walls and other features you remember in the cave. Move toward light and circulating air. If you are carrying a cell phone or watch, use their glowing faces to offer some illumination.

TOUCHING SOMETHING FURRY

Back away slowly. Chances are that the creature you have touched is a hibernating bear. Quietly and carefully backtrack your way through the cave. If you hear noises of the bear(s) starting to wake up, turn and run until you are out of the cave and a good distance away.

STUCK IN NARROW PASSAGE

Slowly exhale to push all the air out of your body, then wiggle back and forth to squeeze your way through the passage. Dig and scrape at the walls of the passage to yield extra room, and strip off clothing and equipment that may be adding to your girth.

Dig at the edges of the rock with any available implement to break the wedge and shift the rock's weight. Use objects such as smaller rocks or sticks to brace the rock away from you. Ration resources and conserve your body heat. Remain calm and control your breathing. Send a companion for help, or, if alone, call out at intervals until rescuers arrive to investigate your disappearance. Always report your plans and expected time of return to others before embarking on an exploration.

HORSEBACK RIDING

HORSE SLIPS OR TRIPS

Calm the horse by talking to it in a soothing voice and patting its neck. If the horse remains skittish, dismount and lead the horse for a short while until it regains its composure. Check the horse's feet to be sure it has not lost a shoe.

CROSSING WATER

Find the surest footing on the bank and let the horse stand on the bank for a few minutes to survey the situation. Ease the horse to the water in a calm manner, giving the horse ample rein and allowing it to proceed at its own pace. Gently squeeze the horse with your legs to nudge it forward, across, and up the other side.

SADDLE SORES

Maintain an equal balance over the saddle and avoid a lot of bumping up and down. Wear long, rugged pants, ideally with some kind of spandex-type underwear underneath, to reduce chaffing.

REARING/BUCKING

Kick your feet out of the stirrups and release the reins. Throw your arms around the neck of the horse as it rears backward. Maintain your grasp and slide around the side of the horse, land on your feet, and push away from the horse to avoid being trampled. This maneuver is known as an emergency dismount.

SURFING

Shark Nearby

Limit your movement to smooth, easy motions. Paddle calmly but immediately back to shore, limiting your splashing to an absolute minimum. Keep sight of the shark at all times. Alert other surfers in the area to the shark's presence.

Battling Territorial Surfers

Wait your turn. Be patient and low-key. Do not drop in on another surfer or cut in on a wave. Surf secondary rather than main peaks. Be deferential without being clueless—competency breeds respect and acceptance.

Wipeout

Let the wave spin you until released—do not try to fight the wave. If you are pushed far under, find the surface by following your leash to your board above.

Unconscious Surfer

Keep the surfer afloat on your board and keep her airway open. Elevate her head as much as possible and paddle back in immediately. Get to the stable environment of shore before attempting to administer CPR.

BOWLING

Rank Rental Shoes

Line the bottom of each shoe with a flat fabric softener sheet. Be sure to tighten the laces so your foot doesn't slide in the shoe.

Fingers Stuck in Ball

Put the ball on the ground and twist your fingers from side-to-side to slip them out. If still stuck, use a little liquid (water is best; not beer or soda) to lubricate the joints of your stuck fingers. If still stuck, obtain grease from a grilled or fried snackbar item and rub it on your fingers as a lubricant. If that doesn't work, dunk the ball and your hand up to the wrist in a tub of ice water, wait for the finger swelling to contract, and free your fingers with a twisting motion.

Ball Dropped on Foot

Remove your bowling shoe and your sock to allow blood to circulate freely to your foot. Recline, elevate the foot over your head, and apply a cold compress. Try wiggling your toes: If difficult, you may have broken a bone, and you should go to the hospital for treatment, being careful not to put weight on the foot. If you can easily move your toes and the pain subsides relatively quickly, apply ice to the area and continue your frame.

DEALING WITH A 7/10 SPLIT

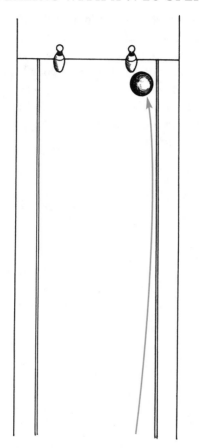

Aim for the far right of the 10 pin if right-handed, the far left of the 7 pin if left-handed. Throw to hit the pin as hard as possible, with significant hook. With luck, the struck pin will bounce off the back wall and knock over the other pin.

Align your left foot with the locator dot if you are right-handed, the right foot if you are left-handed. Square your shoulders to the foul line, and approach your delivery by holding the ball out and back past your hips. Swing the ball like a pendulum toward the pins, keeping your focus on the middle arrow on the lane. Release the ball with your fingers together and follow through with your arm extending toward the pins.

YOGA

Right/Left Confusion

Loosely tie a rubber band around your right wrist, or a shoelace around your left wrist. Remember the mnemonic "rubber band starts with R = right" or "lace starts with L = left."

Slipping on Yoga Mat

Step off your mat and walk to the floorboards closest to the door. Find an area of dust and grit and place your feet and palms down, using the resulting traction to keep yourself firmly in place when you return to the mat.

Bad B.O. Next to You

Dab patchouli or perfume directly under your nostrils. Failing that, breathe in through your mouth and out through your nose.

Passing Gas

Pout your lips and exhale loudly through them at the exact moment you release your gas. Have the sound effect from your mouth continue for a second or two longer than your flatulence. If you draw attention for the noise, look blissful and focused.

STUCK IN PADMASANA

Take a calming breath. Inhale for a count of four, hold for a count of four, and exhale for a count of four, using your heartbeat as the counter.

Slip your closest hand beneath your top foot, placing your other hand below the knee of your top leg. Using the strength of your arms, lift and gently move the leg forward off your thigh and straighten the leg. Use your hands to lift and move your other foot until the leg is straight. Allow your muscles to relax before standing.

Dizzy in Hot Yoga

Leave the hot room and go outside to where the air is cooler. Drink fluids and hold your head between your knees until your dizziness goes away. End your session for the day.

Guru Coming on to You

Flail on every pose in as spasmodic a manner as possible. Whine and complain about each new motion and pretend to cry if anyone says anything to you. At the end of class, inform your guru that, while yoga seems like an acceptable diversion, people who devote their lives to it are obviously just wasting time. Tell him you have to leave early for your white supremacy meeting.

CHAPTER 6

ON THE JOB

IN THE OFFICE

Lay the groundwork for an early departure. As soon as you walk in, circulate the room in a clockwise direction from the entrance, discussing with co-workers a circumstance that will allow for an early exit (your babysitter is double-booked, your pet is sick, you "feel a flu coming on"). If you are enjoying yourself by the time you reach the door again, stay; if not, keep right on walking.

Dealing with Office "Cassanova"

Establish a signal with a co-worker (e.g.: three short coughs) that will indicate that the co-worker should approach and "call you into a meeting" to escape the Cassanova's advances. Keep a personal space buffer of at least two co-workers between you and the Cassanova in all employee group circumstances.

Dealing with Office "Comedian"

Steel yourself for the terrible punchline and gauge your reaction to the level of the Comedian's need for approval, giving no more reaction than is minimally required—a quick groan for puns, an "ah" or "heh" for general purpose responses. Change the subject or walk away immediately.

Awkward Elevator Silence

Mention current weather or temperature, time of day, day of week, month, season, or approaching holiday, and wait for comment. Other subjects of common experience include popular television programs, local sports teams, and the state of being tired. If silence continues, stare at elevator walls or floor until it reaches your destination. Exit immediately.

CLINGY BOSS

Schedule vacations and absences at regular intervals and announce them well in advance. Wean the boss of your presence beforehand by coming in to work early and leaving early—limiting your time in the office with her while still finishing your work. Work extra hard one day, call in sick the next. Your boss will see that your absence does not bring disaster. Be careful not to overdo it, or your boss may decide she doesn't need you at all.

DISTANT BOSS

Loop yourself in on all e-mails and meetings related to your boss's work and discuss projects independently with colleagues to gain a better understanding of details your boss is hiding from you. Read everything that comes out of shared computer printers with her name on it. Display your increased awareness of circumstances to gain her confidence and in turn your inclusion on projects to a deeper level—but be careful what you wish for.

ACTOR/CELEBRITY

Trip on Red Carpet

Turn the bumbling step into a "spontaneous" dance move—the first step of the "Running Man" or a break-dancing lock and pop. Do not look back or glare at the carpet. Smile and keep walking.

Aggressive Paparazzi

Point behind the paparazzi and say "Look it's [actress under 20 years old]!" Turn and move quickly in the opposite direction.

Forgot Award Acceptance Speech

Thank anyone you are usually obligated to spend time with at the holidays: spouse, children, parents, grandparents, great-grandparents, siblings, uncles, aunts, cousins, nephews, nieces, and beloved family pets past and present until the orchestra begins to play, indicating you should "wrap it up" and exit the stage.

Not on Guest List

Quietly whisper to the person next to you in line and ask them to exclaim to the doorman, "Do you know who this is? Do you have any idea who this is?!" Be sure you also whisper your name to the person next to you if you are not certain that he or she, in fact, has any idea who you are.

Agent Won't Return Calls

Call the agency from a phone other than your own, pretending to be the most famous celebrity that your agent handles. Claim that you've just checked yourself into rehab. When the agent answers, identify yourself and demand a meeting in the agent's office, where it will be harder to evade you.

Sex Video Released on Internet

Do nothing. There will be no way to control the situation. Another celebrity sex video is likely to be leaked within weeks that will eclipse the attention paid to yours. Use this time to track down the leak and dispose of any other sensitive or embarrassing material you do not wish to be made public.

MUSICIAN

GUITARIST'S FINGERS BLEED

Apply a thin layer of superglue to your fingertips (also known as the "Stevie Ray Vaughan technique"). Reduce the weight of your string gauge if you feel it will not compromise your music.

TRAPPED UNDER PIANO COLLAPSE

Lie still. Your predicament will be obvious to stagehands and the audience in the front rows, who should come to your aid quickly. A typical baby grand piano weighs around 500 pounds, making it very difficult to move on your own, and in shifting your position you risk further injury. Keep your breathing regular and focus your thoughts. Replay the last few measures of the piece you were performing in your mind as you would in practice.

SMOKE MACHINE MALFUNCTIONS

Keep the house lights low. Gather candles from table seating or the bar and arrange them on the stage. Unplug and play an acoustic set, seated on the stage floor or perched on stools. For your encore, plug in and play electric. Kick over the stool.

Fold a cocktail napkin in half twice lengthwise, then roll to form a cone. Lightly moisten the thin end of the napkin roll in water (not alcohol) and place snugly in the ear opening, leaving at least ½ inch of napkin clear of the ear to grasp and pull out after the concert. Repeat for the other ear.

HECKLERS

Do not respond to the heckler's public taunts or muttered insults. If the heckler is close to the stage, most people in the audience will not have heard anything and any response will call attention to the comment. If the taunt was loudly audible, continue performing without acknowledgment. Even if the crowd has not paid to see you perform, human nature dictates that their sympathy will lie with you. Alternately, learn a few bars of "Free Bird," the song most frequently requested by hecklers, and oblige the request.

LOST YOUR SINGING VOICE

Gargle with saltwater every 3 to 4 hours. Drink herbal tea with lemon and 2 tablespoons of honey afterward, and plenty of water throughout the day. Rest your voice by speaking as little as possible—communicate by writing notes and sending e-mail, IM, or text messages.

SUPERMARKET CLERK

Unattended Child Run Amok

Approach the child and ask if his name is John (or Jake or Jimmy—the name doesn't matter). Once the child corrects you with his name, say "Oh, that's it. I heard someone calling for [child's name] over in the produce aisle." Ask the child who he is with and offer to help find them. When located, politely ask the adult to keep watch over the child.

Bulk-Bin Nibblers

Improvise a task that will keep you proximate to the bulk bins—rearrange cereal boxes front to back, then back to front again. The total average time shoppers spend in a supermarket is about 15 minutes (including checkout time), so you will not need to discourage nibbling with your presence for long before the nibbler's internal shopping clock urges him to move along.

Express-Line Cheat

Check the customer through the line to avoid the confrontation of turning him away to another more appropriate line. As you are ringing up the items, mention that the line has a limit to the number of items and that while you are ringing him through this once, you and the customers who are also waiting in line will appreciate his abiding by the rules in the future.

Pyramid of Oranges Spill

Dive to the floor. Cover as much horizontal ground with your body as you can to prevent oranges from rolling away to far corners of the store. Do not try to control the spill from the top of the display. The pyramid structure as devised in ancient Egypt is inherently stable and will naturally limit the fruit slide.

Customer Paying in Pennies

Spread the pennies out flat on the counter. Place the five fingertips of one hand on the surface of five pennies near the edge of the counter and sweep them in to your other hand and count "five" aloud. Repeat until all pennies have been counted, emptying the noncounting hand into your drawer after every 2 dollars' worth of coins.

Paper Bag Tear

Grab as much of the top edge of the bag lip as possible with your free hand. Set the bag quickly onto the ground, cart bed, or bagging shelf. Open two more shopping bags, one inside the other, aligning the handles, and set it alongside the torn bag. Lifting from the bottom, raise the torn bag with its contents and ease it into the double bag. Heavy duty 70# weight paper gusset (pleated) grocery bags measuring a standard 12" x 7" x 14" can bear a load of 15 pounds if packed evenly and carried gingerly, but you should double-bag if you estimate the load to be more than 10 pounds to protect against torsion as the customer carries it by the handles.

RETAIL SALES CLERK

Monotonous Music Loop

Enlist your co-workers to plant "earworms" in each others' heads by naming songs that stick in mind due to their insidiously catchy melodies. Especially infectious songs include: "Y.M.C.A." by the Village People, "Who Let the Dogs Out," by Baha Men, and "It's a Small World After All."

Sale Scrum

Angle your body sideways to slide between shoppers and move to the edge of the crowd. Try to keep a merchandise rack between yourself and the sought-after items. If you are caught in the mob, keep your arms folded defensively across your chest to protect your breathing area. Stay on your feet or you risk being trampled.

Shoplifter

Watch for attentive behavior—shoplifters will be highly attuned to the activities of employees and other shoppers. Look for bulges in clothing, several layers of clothing, or shoppers who enter the store with seemingly empty bags. Shoppers who walk with strange or jerky movements may also be concealing items. Make your presence known, keep your merchandise well organized so you can detect missing items, and regularly monitor dressing rooms.

Maintaining a Smile

Practice the following sequence in the mirror to strengthen smile muscles, holding each step for 10 seconds: 1) move corners of mouth back, keeping mouth closed; 2) part lips slightly to expose edges of teeth, keeping corners of mouth even; 3) raise cheeks laterally and widen smile—teeth are now fully exposed; 4) relax to step 2; 5) relax to step 1. Repeat several times before your shift to limber up and after your shift to cool down.

Leg Cramp from Standing

Lift and straighten the cramping leg outward to stretch the muscles, pointing the toe, flexing and rotating the ankle. Massage the cramped muscle for 30 seconds. Shake and stamp the leg. Walk it off by pacing for a few minutes. To help stave off cramps, eat calcium-rich foods, avoid drinking soft drinks, and flex and rotate your legs and ankles once an hour. Stretch your muscles by performing deep knee bends and touching your toes.

BARTENDER

BAR FIGHT

Alert the bouncer and call the police. Tell nearby patrons to keep away from the fight. Do not attempt to break up the fight yourself—one or both of the fighters may be armed.

PATRON MAKES UNWANTED ADVANCES

Claim you are married, but that you remove your wedding band so you don't scratch the glasses while washing them. Offer to introduce the patron to other single customers in the bar if you're reasonably sure the introduction will be well received by both parties. Beware that you run the risk of hearing both sides of the breakup story if things don't work out.

PATRON USES YOU AS SHRINK

Let the patron talk. Nod sympathetically. When asked for advice, rephrase the question as a question for the patron ("Well, what do *you* think?") and always agree with the customer. Solicit the input of other bar patrons, who will likely be free with their advice. Offer no opinions of your own or you will leave yourself open for updates. Make a show of keeping busy—cleaning glasses, cutting garnishes, and refilling the snack bowls—to avoid getting sucked in.

Flaming Cocktail Fire

Throw a wet bar rag onto the flames and spray water from the fountain hose to fight a flaming cocktail fire that has spilled and spread onto the bar. Advise patrons to step back.

Nod to waiting customers to acknowledge them and say "I'll be with you in a second." Glance up and down the bar to take notice of the order in which the customers have arrived and try to tend to them in roughly that order. Take multiple orders at once, and think ahead for ways to consolidate actions and multitask. Start a beer pouring from the tap while reaching for a liquor bottle for another drink, and line up multiple drinks with the same base liquor for double pours. Always use both hands. Be sure all garnishes are precut at the beginning of your shift.

WAITER

Spilled Tray of Food

Apologize profusely if the food landed on a customer and alert the manager; he should make an offer on behalf of the restaurant to pick up the dry cleaning tab. Meals affected by the spilled food should be replaced, and a free dessert offered to any nearby customers.

Table with Messy Baby

Ignore the mess at the table until the family with the baby leaves. If the mess is affecting other diners, offer to reseat them, or use a carpet sweeper or broom/dustpan to clean the area around their table.

Non-Tippers

Ask the customer if there was a problem with the food or the service. Say "Is there something we could have done better to make your meal more enjoyable?"

Table Doesn't Pay

Run after the customers and say they've "forgotten" to pay the check, giving them the benefit of the doubt. If they refuse or run, call the police.

Wrong Order Placed

Cancel the incorrect order, then tell the kitchen you need the new order "on the fly," or right away.

Slow Kitchen

Apologize to your customers for the delay, but do not make excuses. Offer a round of drinks on the house.

Food Critic Arrives

Do not publicly acknowledge the critic in any way. On your next naturally occurring trip to the kitchen, alert the manager and chef. The manager should alert the other waitstaff as they return to the kitchen. They should be on their best behavior, but also not acknowledge the critic's presence as anything out of the ordinary.

Restaurant Is Mob Front

Stay as far as possible from any card games. Do not "ask permission" to use the toilet.

ZOO KEEPER

PANDAS WON'T MATE

Close the panda house and separate the male and female bears at the first sign the female has gone into heat. Reunite the pair when she is at peak fertility, which lasts for approximately 2 days per year. Meanwhile, show the male panda videos of other pandas mating to teach the proper behavior.

LLAMA SPITTING

Allow the llama to calm down by keeping away from the animal for 15 to 20 minutes and advising patrons to do the same. Llamas spit to express displeasure, and will spit at other llamas as well as at humans. Move away if you notice the llama's ears back and nose up, signals that the llama may be ready to spit. If the problem is recurring, post a sign near the llama enclosure alerting zoo patrons to the llama's sensitivities.

KICKED BY ZEBRA

Move back: Zebras kick with their hind legs when they are followed too closely, or with the front legs as a defensive measure. The zebra's powerful hindquarters can deliver a kick with force sufficient to break a crocodile's jaw.

ON THE JOB

MONKEYS ESCAPE

Secure the enclosure breach. Lure the monkeys back to their enclosure with ripe bananas, oranges, or other special treats, offering food by hand as well as in the cage. The benefit of recapturing them quickly will outweigh having "rewarded" their escape behavior. Use a tranquilizer if the monkeys refuse to return to their habitat.

Petting-Zoo Bite

Wash the bite with soap and water, lathering for 5 minutes even if the skin is not visibly broken. Apply pressure to stop any bleeding, then apply an antiseptic (iodine, chlorhexidine, or alcohol). If skin is broken, encourage the patron to visit a doctor to be sure that they do not need a rabies or a tetanus booster.

CHAPTER 7

TRAVEL

ON SAFARI

LIONS

Get inside a closed-top vehicle, roll up all windows, and drive to a safe location as quickly as possible. Lions typically will not attack humans unless starving or threatened, but they should be considered a danger when encountered in the wild. Lions may attack from any position and will enter water and climb trees in search of prey.

CHARGING RHINO

Run to and climb the nearest tree, raising yourself at least 6 feet off the ground—the height to which a rhino can typically strike with its horn. If you cannot get to a tree, run for thick scrub brush and get in as far as possible. If no other options are available, stand your ground, face the rhino, and shout. Rhinos may veer from loud noises.

HYENAS

Move children and infirm or elderly members of your party indoors or into a closed-top vehicle if you hear animal noises such as grunting, growling, giggling, or screaming, or notice hyenas advancing in groups of two or more. Though they are known as scavengers, hyenas are opportunistic predators and may attack humans if they sense an advantage in size or number. Avoid areas with fresh kills, especially at night, when hyenas typically hunt.

STAMPEDE OF GIRAFFES

Wade into the nearest body of water. Giraffes typically avoid water except for drinking. If you cannot reach water, climb a tree or seek available shelter. The giraffes' large hooves pose your most immediate danger.

IN THE JUNGLE

Lost in Jungle

Follow the path of a river: Most jungle settlements are on or near rivers. As you walk, turn over fresh vegetation to mark your trail, should you need to backtrack. Break up termite mounds and rub the dirt on your skin as a natural insect repellent.

Stalked by Leopard

Cross a river or other body of water to throw the leopard off your scent trail. Note that the water is not a safe area in itself—leopards hunt fish and are excellent swimmers. Leopards typically observe prey from trees and stay well hidden when stalking, so also avoid areas with large numbers of rodents or other small mammals that might be under surveillance.

Boa Constrictor

Do not struggle with or strike at the boa—it will only tighten its grip. Slowly and carefully uncoil the boa, from whichever end is within reach. If you attempt to control the head, hold it well away from your body to avoid being bitten—all snakes, including boas, have teeth.

DRINKING WATER FROM A VINE

Cut a deep notch in the vine as high up as you can reach. Cut the vine off as low as possible below the initial cut and let water drip into a container or your mouth. When dripping stops, make another cut at the top of the vine and repeat until the vine is drained. This method will work on any vine, though not all vines yield palatable water.

Select a thick green vine, or braid 3 or more slender vines to create a rope. Pull the vine sharply and test that it will support your full weight. Keeping both hands securely around the vine at all times, back up as far as possible, then run and leap toward the place you wish to swing. Only release your grip on the swinging vine if you are completely over your target area.

IN THE DESERT

Runaway Camel

Pull the reins gently but steadily in the direction the camel's head is pointing. Do not jerk or pull the reins straight back. If there is a saddle, hold on to the horn. The camel will eventually slow to a trot in the direction of the reins. Turn the reins further inward to walk the camel into a circle and stop. Jump off and keep hold of the reins.

Sandstorm

Wet a bandana and place it over your nose and mouth, then cover your head with a T-shirt or towel. Move to higher—even slightly higher—ground, or take available shelter such as the leeward side of a slope or hill. Turn your back to the storm direction. If you have and can reach a vehicle, back it into the wind to avoid pitting of the windshield.

Finding Water

Dig with a flat rock or other implement around fresh vegetation, in dry streambeds, or visibly damp areas where animals may have scratched to reach ground water. Wipe plants with a bandana or cloth to collect dew; wring out and drink the moisture. Watch for and follow birds, which may congregate near watering holes in arid land.

The sun rises in the east and sets in the west. Clouds and weather patterns generally, but do not always, move from west to east. In the northern hemisphere, the sun is in the southern sky. At night, the last star in the handle of the Big Dipper constellation is the North Star: walking in its direction leads north. In the southern hemisphere, the sun is in the northern sky. At night, look for the Southern Cross—four bright stars in the constellation of a tilted cross. Walking toward a point 5 times the length of the longest axis leads south.

JEEP STUCK IN SAND

Reduce air pressure in the tires by half. Jack up the vehicle, then pile sand under the wheels without traction. Tamp down the sand so it is compressed (wet it if sufficient water is available), then place sand ladders, floor mats, or anything else at hand under the wheels to provide traction. Lower the truck, reduce the load and passengers, and drive out slowly.

IN THE WOODS

ANKLE SPRAIN ON TRAIL

Tear a T-shirt into long, 4-inch-wide strips. Immobilize the ankle by wrapping it in a figure-eight pattern, up and over the ankle and back around the foot. Use a stout piece of wood to support your weight on the injured side. If the ankle is badly swollen, soak it in cold water for 15 minutes before wrapping.

ARM CAUGHT UNDER BOULDER

Push gently against the boulder with your free hand or by pressing your feet against it. Gently try to move the boulder in all directions. If the boulder does not move, cool the area of the arm under the boulder with ice to constrict blood vessels, then try to remove. If no ice is available, apply lip balm to the arm and carefully slide it out.

BIGFOOT SIGHTING

Remain still. If you are carrying a camera, slowly retrieve it, use manual (not digital) zoom setting, and take as many photos at the highest resolution possible. The creature will likely flee quickly once it is aware of your presence. Do not pursue—it may behave unpredictably if chased. Take note of the creature's physical and behavioral traits, including height, smell, and speed and posture of movement. Photograph any footprints and mark the location so you can return later to take a casting of the prints.

THINGS YOU CAN EAT

Mallow: Eat leaves.

Wild strawberry: Eat berries.

Chicory: Eat raw leaves, and boiled root. New leaves are best.

Dandelion: Eat stems, leaves, flowers, and/or root.

Prickly pear: Remove outer skin and spines; eat pads and fruits.

FENDING OFF A PACK OF WOLVES

Charge a member of the pack to scare it and the others away from you. Throw sticks or rocks at the wolf closest to you. Wolves tend to attack the legs of their prey—kick out at any wolf that gets too close.

BEARS

Back away slowly upon sighting any bear or cub. Do not run—this may draw attention and you cannot outrun a bear. Do not climb a tree: Most bears will either climb trees or swat at an object in them. If the bear charges, curl to the ground and play dead. If the bear attacks, strike sensitive areas such as the bear's eyes and nose with a rock, stick, or your hands. When hiking in bear country, wear bear bells or sing or whistle.

MAKING A SMOKE SIGNAL

Pile and burn dry grass, wet leaves, or an abandoned car tire in a clearing, continuing to feed the fire to create a smoke column that will be visible for miles. Strive for a consistent quantity of smoke—do not attempt to send a "message" by covering and uncovering the fire with a blanket, which risks smothering the flames or setting fire to the blanket. Await help.

AT THE BEACH

BITTEN BY CRAB

Place the crab back into the water to get it to release its grip. If the crab will not release its grip, pry its claw loose with your free hand and fling the crab away. It is very hard to pry a crab's claw apart. If the skin is broken, treat the injury as you would any puncture wound: Clean and dress, using antibacterial ointment.

MOBILE PHONE FALLS IN WATER

Remove the phone from the water as quickly as possible and turn it off. Hold the phone so the keypad is facing toward the sand and remove the back cover. Take out the battery and dry it and all battery contacts thoroughly with a clean cloth or T-shirt. Remove the front cover and keypad. Using a hair dryer, blow hot air into the phone for at least 10 minutes. Allow the phone to dry overnight or longer, then attempt to switch it on.

SEVERE SUNBURN

Get out of the sun immediately. Place strips of cool, wet cloth over the burn area and leave in place. Never put ice directly on bare skin or you risk freezing skin cells. Remove the cloths as they warm, apply a topical burn gel such as aloe vera, and re-cover with chilled cloths. Take an over-the-counter pain reliever as necessary. Stay indoors, or, if impossible, completely out of the sun.

SAND IN SWIMSUIT

Wade into the ocean. Pull your suit away from your body, jump up and down, and shimmy from side to side to allow trapped sand to be washed away.

Heatstroke

Immerse yourself in cold water. If immersion is impossible, spray yourself with cool water while fanning the skin. Stop cooling when body temperature falls below 102°F and seek medical assistance.

Lost Sunglasses

Borrow a mask and snorkel and check on the sea floor in the area where you were swimming most recently. Check under towel edges. Check on top of your head.

Emergency Sunshade

Lay a towel between the backs of two beach chairs, or dig a deep depression in the sand, cover it with a towel, and crawl in. Alternately, cover your body with wet sand. Re-wet the mound as the sand dries to maintain coating.

Stung by Jellyfish

Rinse the skin with seawater only—freshwater will make the sting worse. Pour white vinegar on the wound area to prevent additional toxins from being released, then remove the tentacles. Take an over-the-counter pain medication as necessary. Urinating on the wound is not an effective treatment; it may actually cause the nematocysts (stinging cells) to fire secondary venom.

Sand Flies

Stay in a windy area or sit in the path of a fan. Sand flies typically will not bite when there is a breeze or rapid airflow. The flies are also attracted to body heat—keep skin cool with frequent swimming.

Riptide

Swim parallel to shore, perpendicular to the current, for 25 to 50 yards, or until you are no longer being pulled out to sea. Do not try to fight the current by swimming directly to shore.

Hurricane

Immediately evacuate coastal areas to avoid storm surge, then get indoors. Avoid buildings with eaved roofs and exterior windows not covered by plywood. Remain in a windowless room at the center of the structure until the storm passes.

Tsunami

Move to high ground quickly, 40 to 50 feet above sea level, or to the fifth floor of a building. Climb a tree or low rooftop only as a last resort. Warning signs of an approaching tsunami include water quickly rushing out to sea, a loud roar, and shaking ground.

ON THE ROAD

OVERHEATING ENGINE

Put heat and blowers on full strength to draw hot air away from the engine. Pull over as soon as possible. Turn off the car and allow the engine and radiator to cool for at least 30 minutes. Cover your hand with a large, thick piece of cloth and slowly open the coolant reservoir cap. Add coolant or a combination of water and coolant mixed to a 1:1 ratio and drive to a service station, keeping heat and blowers on full power.

CHILDREN FIGHTING IN BACKSEAT

Distract bickering children and play on their competitive nature to see who can spot colors or types of cars or license plates first. Play yourself to increase their interest, but let them win or you risk their sulking. Do not threaten to pull the car over unless you are prepared to follow through on the threat. If you must pull over, do so at a rest stop or another safe location, never on the shoulder. Once stopped, let them run around to wear them out.

CARSICK CHILD

Stop the car. Walk around with the child for several minutes, or until nausea passes. To prevent car sickness, adjust the child's seating position so he can see out the window. Remove reading material and handheld video games, and offer small snacks to distract from any symptoms.

FALLING ASLEEP AT THE WHEEL

Open windows to bring fresh air into the car. Turn the radio up to a volume louder than you're normally comfortable with, to a news or talk radio station (human voices may draw alert attention better than rhythmic or repetitive music, even if it is loud). Drinking coffee will keep you awake but may make you jittery and force frequent bathroom stops, prolonging your time in the car. Even a very brief cat nap in a safe area should make you feel more awake and refreshed.

FLOODED ENGINE

Hold the accelerator pedal to the floor and turn the key to the "start" position. If the engine does not turn over, keep the pedal to the floor, turn the ignition off, then turn it back on. Repeat until the cars starts. Once the engine turns over, release the pedal. The engine will run rough until the excess fuel is burned. Drive only after the engine runs normally. Use this method only for older cars with a carburetor and without fuel injection.

BRAKE FAILURE

Continue pumping the brakes to build pressure with any remaining brake fluid. Shift the car into the lowest gear possible. Gently pull up on the emergency brake using even, constant pressure, and steer the car to the shoulder as it slows to a stop.

DEER IN THE HEADLIGHTS

Brake firmly and blow your horn with one long blast to frighten the deer into action. Do not swerve or you will confuse the deer about which way to run. If you hit the deer, do not touch the animal; move the car off the road, set the hazard lights, and call the police. Drive using high beams whenever possible on dark wooded roads.

Ditching Psychotic Hitchhiker

Pull over at the first populated area, preferably an active gas station or truck stop with people visible outside. If the hitchhiker will not get out, take the keys and leave the car, then get help. Do not drive down a deserted country lane or to an abandoned farmhouse.

Evading a Maniac Trucker

Take a tight-radius turn at high speed: The trucker should be unable to follow. If available, call the toll-free number printed on the truck to report the trucker's dangerous driving—include the license plate number—or simply call the company office's main number and ask to make a complaint.

Talking Your Way Out of a Ticket

Apologize and ask for a warning. Do not make excuses for your behavior. Do not directly answer leading questions ("Do you know how fast you were going?" "Do you know why I stopped you?") since your responses may be taken as an admission of guilt, and you should plead not guilty if you cannot get out of the ticket. Instead, say "I'm not sure, officer."

Black Ice Skid

Remove your foot from the accelerator. Do not brake. As you feel the wheels regain traction, slowly turn the steering wheel in the direction you want the car to move. Do not make sudden movements of the wheel. Drive using low headlight beams during an ice- or snowstorm to increase visibility.

Fire Under Hood

Pull over, turn the engine off, and get out as quickly as possible. Do not open the hood. Move to a safe location at least 100 yards from the burning vehicle and call for emergency help.

Flat Tire

Remove the hubcap and loosen the lug nuts or bolts while the tire is firmly on the ground. Set the jack under the jacking point just in front of the tire for a rear flat or just behind it for a front flat. Jack the car up. Remove the wheel and replace with the spare. Tighten the bolts slightly. Lower the car and finish tightening the bolts one after the other in a star pattern while the wheel is held stable by the weight of the car against the ground.

CAMPING

Rain

Set up your tarp at the first sign of rain. If your tent has rain flies, set a tarp under the tent to keep the ground under the tent dry. If your tent does not have a rain fly, set up the tent and put the tarp on top of it to keep the tent from saturating. Do not set camp in depressions, gullies, and other low spots where rainwater is likely to collect. Always seal your tent with seam sealer 24 hours before packing the tent for a camping trip.

Snow

Clear snow and ice from the tent site, if it is possible to do so. If clearing the snow is impossible, pile dry leaves under your tent before setting it up. A domed tent should prevent snow from accumulating on the tent roof and causing collapse. For further insulation, or if you don't have a domed tent, set up a weather fly by hanging or staking a tarp above the tent so that two sides rise higher than the others at an angle to allow snow to slide away from the tent. Drive plastic tent stakes into firm ground, or use steel spikes for ice. Don extra layers of clothing.

TRAVEL

Animal Proofing

Establish camp at a remote, empty site: Animals accustomed to people are less afraid of them and may expect to find food in well-trafficked areas. Hang food and all cooking utensils from tree branches several feet off the ground. Leave your packs unzipped to prevent foraging animals from tearing them open in search of food odors. Keep all food items in a car, if available. Never keep food inside your tent.

Snake in Sleeping Bag

Pick up the sleeping bag from the bottom and dump the snake outside. If you are in the bag and feel a snake, avoid sudden movements. Very slowly work the bag down toward your feet as you pull your upper body and then legs out. Keep the bag rolled up and tied when you are not using it to prevent snakes from entering, and keep your tent flaps zipped.

Rattlesnake Bite

Wash the bite area with soap and water, then immobilize the bite area, keeping it lower than your heart. If you are more than 30 minutes from emergency medical care, wrap a bandage 2 to 4 inches above the bite to help slow the venom. The bandage should not cut off blood flow: It should be loose enough for a finger to slip underneath. Do not make incisions near the bite or attempt to suck out the venom.

Construct a bow by running a taut piece of string between the ends of a sapling. Place a stick against and perpendicular to the string and twist so the string loops once around the stick. Holding the bow with one hand, place the bottom of the stick on a piece of dry wood. Holding a finger on either side of the stick to keep it in place, quickly move the bow back and forth, turning the stick and creating friction. Add straw or dry pine needles to the bottom of the stick as it heats up, until they catch fire.

ON A CRUISE

SEASICKNESS

Move to the center of the ship, as close to the water line as possible, but in a location with good fresh air circulation. Face your direction of travel and focus on an unmoving object in the distance, such as the horizon. Ginger drinks may help to settle the stomach, and prescription or over-the-counter seasickness remedies, particularly the scopolamine patch, may help with nausea. Rehydrate with water or sports drinks if vomiting occurs.

CREW MUTINY

Avoid revealing your allegiances and keep all options on the table. Do not sit at the captain's table. Do not fraternize with the crew. Stay away from the ship's lower decks, where crew members are quartered, to reduce risk of being captured and used as a hostage.

SINKING SHIP

Put on warm clothing (long pants and a long-sleeve shirt) in case you are exposed to seawater. Never evacuate a cruise ship unless you are expressly told to do so by the crew: You are much more likely to be found with the ship than in the water. Stay on the ship and wait for rescue. Large ships take hours or days to sink, so help should arrive before the ship sinks. Put on a life jacket and wait for further instructions from the crew.

OPENING A COCONUT ON A DESERT ISLAND

Drive the end of a stick into the ground and sharpen the top end.
Slam the nut down on the point of the stick, using both hands to crack
the outer fibrous covering. Smash the inner shell against a rock or tree.

Fallen Overboard

Immediately yell "Man overboard, [port/starboard] side!" as loud as you can. The port side is the left side of the boat, as you face toward the bow (front). Wave your arms as high as you can to attract attention, and keep yelling. If you spot someone overboard, shout the same thing, throw a life preserver, and point at the person in the water until help arrives.

Norwalk Virus Outbreak

Wash your hands with soap and warm water frequently. Use disposable wipes, tissue paper, or paper towels when touching doorknobs, elevator buttons, toilet handles, faucets, light switches, and other objects handled by other people. Only eat food that is prepackaged and sealed or that is thoroughly cooked to 160°F for red meat or 180°F for whole poultry. Avoid eating raw foods. Drink only bottled water, or bottled or canned juice, soft drinks, or milk that you have opened yourself. Remain in your cabin and limit contact with other passengers and crew for the duration of the cruise.

BY AIR

Impending Crash

Quickly make a mental note of the nearest exit, keeping in mind that it may be behind you. Buckle your seatbelt and remove high heels to avoid puncturing the emergency slide (if you are over water). Lean forward and place your head in your lap, then cover it with your arms. Follow instructions from the crew.

Severe Turbulence

Secure your seatbelt and look out the nearest window, focusing on the horizon. If the horizon is not visible, focus on a fixed object within the plane, which will be rising and falling at the same rate you are, to reduce the sensation of violent motion.

Jet Lag

Upon boarding the plane, set your watch to your destination time zone and follow the appropriate eating and sleeping schedule. Drink water to stay hydrated, and avoid coffee or alcohol while on board. Remove contact lenses and wear glasses to prevent drying of eyes. Wear loose clothing in layers so you can adjust to the temperature of the cabin. On arrival, keep yourself awake by staying outside and busy during the day and turn in no more than an hour or two earlier than you normally would.

Muscle Cramps

Get up once per hour and walk through the cabin to increase blood flow to muscles. Perform 5 to 10 deep knee bends and stretches in the galleys or near the lavatory. While seated, extend your legs as far as possible under the seat in front of you—lean the seat back for added reach. Remove your shoes, rotate your ankles, and flex your toes.

Canceled Flight

Call the airline's reservation system (or, better, your travel agent) on a mobile phone while waiting in line for rebooking; you may be able to get a new reservation before you reach the ticket desk. When possible, use a paper ticket, which can be endorsed to a different airline more easily than an electronic ticket.

Chatty Neighbor

Put on headphones or feign sleep until your neighbor gets the message. If you are in a row with three or more adjacent seats, get up and spend 10 or more minutes in the lavatory area of the plane, encouraging the chatty flyer to begin talking to the other person in your row.

BY BUS

Sleeping on Overnight Bus

Secure a window seat so that you can curl up against the side of the bus. Support your head with a neck pillow or a rolled-up sweater. Wear earplugs or noise-canceling headphones from a music player. Fashion emergency earplugs from rolled-up toilet paper (leave at least an inch of the paper outside of the ear canal for easy removal). Wear an eye mask or dark sunglasses, or tie socks around your head and across your eyes. Do not sit near the lavatory.

Arm Stuck in Door

Pound on the door with your free hand. Yell "door!" (Yelling "help" or "hey" will delay assistance.) Continue pounding and shouting. If you are outside the bus, drop any luggage and run alongside if possible until the bus stops.

Standing on Overcrowded Bus

Remove and carry backpacks before boarding, and stand with them resting on the floor and clutched between your feet and ankles once aboard. Slide a purse or camera around to the front of your person and keep one hand resting on it and holding the strap. If you are able to slide your bag, briefcase, or luggage beneath the seat of a sitting passenger and stand alongside, keep contact with the bag by touching it with your feet at all times.

SHARING SPACE WITH LIVESTOCK

Keep your arms close to your sides. Hold a book or magazine open and in a defensive position, ready to deflect an errant wing or pecking beak. Tie long hair back. Keep food items stowed away.

AT A MUSEUM

MUSEUM LEGS

Stand on your tiptoes, extend your arms above your head, stretch as far as possible, and hold for 5 seconds. Slowly return to flat footing. Repeat 5 times. Standing with your legs 2 to 3 feet apart, bend your torso backward at the waist, then extend forward and attempt to touch the ground with your fingertips. Repeat. Note: These stretches will also relieve "museum back." Limit duration of art viewing to 2 hour intervals.

MANET OR MONET?

If you cannot get close enough to read the museum tag: Paintings of water lilies, hay stacks, cathedrals, bridges, or gardens are probably Monet. Paintings of a naked woman on a bed or at a picnic, a bar girl, a flute player, or French people in boats are probably Manet. Girls in frilly dresses holding umbrellas are a toss-up.

EYESTRAIN

Close your eyes and cover them lightly with your palms to block out light. Hold for 30 seconds, taking long, deep breaths. Resume museum viewing. At every sixth piece of artwork, blink lightly and quickly 10 times in succession.

Overcrowded Exhibition

Begin at the end of the exhibition, where crowds will be thinner, and work backward. Approach crowded works of art from the side, stepping closer to the artwork in small shuffling increments. Keep your arms crossed in front of you, elbows out, to prevent your chest from being compressed in the crowd crush.

Bored Child

Make a game out of noticing things that have nothing to do with the exhibition. Ask the child to count the number of people in the crowd who are wearing boots or black clothing. Promise to visit a part of the museum the child will enjoy more (mummies, dinosaurs) or leave the museum entirely after a short, set period of time—say, 10 minutes more. Give updates every few minutes and pick up your viewing pace. Leaving on an upbeat note will make it more likely you'll be able to take the child to museums later on without resistance.

AT AN AMUSEMENT PARK

STUCK ON RIDE

Test the safety bar, strap, or harness to ensure it is still operational. If suspended upside down, fold the tops of your pockets upward and tuck in around any valuable items such as keys, wallet, or mobile phone to hold in place. Do not attempt to exit the ride. Await help.

SICK ON RIDE

Fight the urge to be sick until the ride reaches the outside edge of a turn or the apogee of a climb. Face in the opposite direction of the motion of the ride and vomit over the side of the car or into a corner on the floor of an enclosed car. Keep your eyes on a fixed point and your hands on the safety rail to reduce your perception of motion until the ride ends. Report the incident to a ride attendant.

LONG LINES

Enter the park as soon as it opens in the morning and move immediately to the most popular rides first, consulting maps and brochures to plot the path of maximum efficiency. Visit popular rides at dinnertime, when lines are generally shorter. Make use of any appointment-time ticketing options made available by the park. Visit the park on a weekday while school is in session, if possible.

COSTUMED MASCOT INSISTS ON HUG

Keep a bench or child between yourself and the mascot. Shout "No!" and the mascot's name, if known. If unable to escape, crouch low to the ground, as the heavy plush fur of the mascot's suit may prevent him from bending down.

FOOD

Food Is Too Spicy

Eat rice or bread to help remove spicy oils from your mouth. Suck on a lime or consume fruit juice containing citric acid, which acts as a solvent to pepper oil, or swish a small amount of an alcoholic beverage around in your mouth. Dairy products will also help neutralize hot oils. Water will not help—oil and water do not mix.

Presented with Exotic but Distasteful Delicacy

Cut the food into small pieces. Breathe through your mouth, not your nose, as you place the first piece into your mouth. Immediately move the food to the rear of your tongue where flavor receptors are less sensitive. If possible, swallow without chewing. Repeat until at least half the item has been consumed to avoid giving offense to your hosts.

Food Poisoning

Vomit and use the bathroom as necessary. Avoid taking antidiarrhea medications, which may prolong the presence of the pathogen in the gut. To replace electrolytes, consume sports drinks or make a rehydration drink: Mash a banana and mix it with 1 quart of water, $1/2$ teaspoon of baking soda, and $1/2$ teaspoon of salt. Repeat every few hours or until the sickness fades.

Drink plenty of water to replace lost fluids. Take an over-the-counter antibacterial medication, if available. Lacto-bacillus bacteria (acidophilus and bulgaricus) are also effective: Drink fermented milk, such as buttermilk, and eat yogurt, which contains bulgaricus. Remain close to clean and convenient restroom facilities. Symptoms should pass in several days' time.

SAFELY ORDER WHEN YOU DON'T SPEAK THE LANGUAGE

Point to item(s) you wish to order. Point to slash-through and any item you do not wish to order.

NO

mushrooms

chicken

garlic

fish

tomato

pork

chile peppers

onion

goat

broccoli

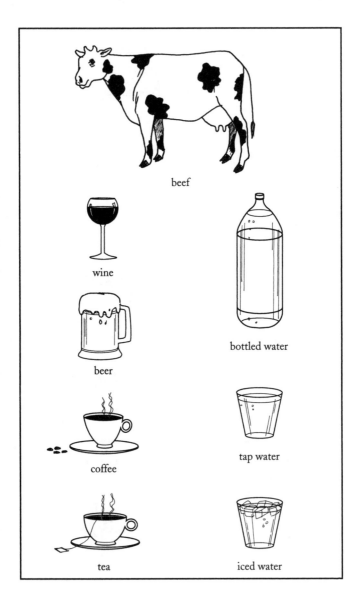

beef

wine

beer

coffee

tea

bottled water

tap water

iced water

noodles

shrimp

egg

toast

fruit

pizza

hamburger

french fries

CHAPTER 8

RELATIONSHIPS
& FAMILY

MATE

Caught Noticing an Attractive Stranger

Think fast—point out an item of the stranger's clothing and mention to your partner that you think the color, style, or cut would look nice on her. Alternately, point out (or plausibly make up) a flaw in the stranger's appearance, such as crossed eyes, bitten fingernails, a weird mole, or buck teeth, and ask if your partner noticed it, too.

Hates Favorite TV Show

Force your mate to watch a show so bad even you can't stand it. Say it is your favorite show of all time and ask your mate to understand how important it is to you and your relationship. Then compromise slightly and tell your mate you won't make her watch the truly awful show so long as you can watch your (real) favorite show instead.

Won't Do Chores

Divide duties and post the list on your refrigerator. Tell your mate that every time you do one of his chores, he has to pay you for the service. Stagger the payments depending on the nature of the job: Taking out the trash might cost him $5, while cleaning the kitty litter is $10, and raking all the leaves outside is $20. Use this money to buy yourself extravagant lunches and clothes.

WON'T LEAVE HOUSE

Host a gender-stereotypical night to drive your spouse away. If female, invite "the girls" over to watch weepy films, gossip, and eat guilt-inducing snacks. If male, bring "the boys" over for an evening of cigar smoking, poker, whiskey, and sports argument. Once you have laid precedent, you can drive your spouse away at any time by announcing another "girl's night," but without having to actually host such an event.

PARENTS

Unannounced Arrival

Quickly make a hotel reservation—for yourself. Tell your parents you're extremely happy that they've come, because now you can cancel the housesitter you'd scheduled for your weekend trip to the ocean/lake/desert. Give your parents a detailed list of all the things that need to be monitored and taken care of while you're away (plants, lawn, dog/cat/fish/gerbils, kids), pack your bag, and leave.

Critical of Lifestyle

Ascertain some of your parents' personal heroes, be they musicians, artists, political figures, or athletes. Study the childhoods of these people until you find one with an off-beat lifestyle choice—ideally, similar to your own, but barring that, at least peculiar. Cite this example whenever your parents raise their complaints.

Condescending

Fight fire with fire. Lord over them any advantage you may have, be it age/looks/physicality or freedom/irresponsibility. Serve them "underappreciated" wine gleefully and take them to esoteric, complex foreign movies by directors whose names are eight syllables with a single vowel.

Rude to Your Mate

Call your parents and tearfully explain that your mate is considering dumping you because of them. Say that you only hope you are never as mean-spirited with your own children, whom they will never meet as long as they keep up that kind of behavior.

Pressure to Have Grandkids

Take in a few dogs and cats from the local animal shelter. When your parents come to visit your menagerie, explain that you are preparing yourself for eventual parenthood by taking care of other lifeforms first, as you've read it's an excellent preparation for children of your own. Ask your parents to animal sit as much as possible.

Nag You to Move Home

Tell your parents you're really thinking about it because then you won't have to work or cook/clean, and you could fully devote yourself to online poker tournaments.

Call Three Times a Day

Ditch your current phone number and get a new one without telling them about it. Have your voicemail set to pick up after the smallest amount of rings possible, or cancel it altogether (tell your parents it's a cost-cutting move). If possible, assign your parents their own ringtone so you don't accidentally take their calls.

BABY

CRIES WHEN YOU PICK UP

Hold the baby close to your chest so it can hear your heart beat as you gently rock it back and forth. As you do this, hum low notes so that the buzz reverberates in your throat and chest. If this fails, place the baby in a basket, put the basket on top of your dryer, and turn it on. The resultant noise and rhythm will lull the baby into sleep.

POOPS WHEN YOU'RE HOLDING

Keep the baby at arm's length. Turn your face to the side and breathe through your mouth. Holding the baby firmly under its arms, hand it to the nearest available adult and exit the room.

INTRODUCING SOLID FOOD

Give the baby a plastic baby spoon to play with so she becomes accustomed to its feel. Mix rice cereal with milk or water in a 1 to 3 ratio until the mixture is smooth and runny. Fill half the baby spoon with the mixture and gently put it in the baby's mouth. With your patience, the baby will learn to keep the food in her mouth and swallow it rather than push it out with her tongue. Gradually give the baby more solid food, keeping track of what she likes and dislikes, and go with what she enjoys.

Diaper Rash

Clean the area thoroughly with water, without wiping, and let the baby "air out" before applying a zinc-based diaper cream. To prevent diaper rash, change the baby's diaper frequently, and quickly after defecation.

Teething Discomfort

Give the baby a cold teething ring. Store the ring in the refrigerator or freezer when it is not in use. You may also give the baby cold applesauce or yogurt. If the gums appear to be inflamed, wipe them gingerly with a dampened piece of gauze.

Won't Sleep at Night

Develop a very specific routine for putting the baby to bed: It can be as simple as a feeding, a story book, and a lullabye at a given time of the evening. If the baby still won't sleep, you may either do your best to ignore the baby's crying; or you may pick the baby up, comfort him, and put him in bed with you. Warning: Most parents believe very strongly in one of these solutions and are irrationally hostile to practitioners of the other solution. Don't ever tell anyone how you get your baby to sleep at night.

CHILD

"I Hate You"

Acknowledge her behavior and feelings by pointing them out to her without judgment ("I can tell you are angry that you can't have ice cream because you are screaming at me.") If the problem is that she can't have something she wants, offer a choice of other permissible items or activities. Do not take the "hatred" personally—children experience emotions as all-encompassing from moment to moment, but such outbursts have no bearing on how she really feels about you.

Thumbsucking

Praise your child when she refrains from the habit. Talk to her often about how she is harming her teeth by continuing to suck her thumb. If this doesn't work, wrap the thumb in adhesive tape or a glove, or tape a tongue depressor to the thumb so it won't be flexible (and it therefore won't provide the comfort the child is seeking).

Always Asks "Why"

Resist the temptation to just say "because." Ask the child what he thinks the answer is if you grow weary of supplying answers yourself (or if you don't actually know the answer). You may be amazed and entertained by the results. Write his questions down and find out the answers together by visiting a library or a museum.

HYPER FROM SUGAR BUZZ

Take your child to a playground obstacle course and convince him to break the course's "world record" (make up a ridiculously short time). At the end of each run, announce that he is closer to beating the record and ask him to run it again. At signs of exhaustion, proclaim the record broken and take the child home to bed. Tame subsequent sugar buzzes by asking the child to return to defend his title against "challengers."

Won't Go to Sleep

Sit on the bed with your child and, in a soothing voice, talk him through the process of relaxing each part of his body. If that fails, take him with you to watch late-night talk shows, infomercials, and made-for-TV movies until he can't take it anymore and goes back to bed on his own.

Won't Take a Bath

Spray boys with ultra-feminine perfume and girls with a smear of Marmite. Explain that the only way to get rid of those odors is by soaking in a tub for several minutes and using the soap and shampoo. If your child appreciates and/or is unconcerned about those smells, say that you know for a fact that the child's favorite cartoon character always bathes at night.

New-Sibling Jealousy

Give your child some responsibility toward the new baby. Make it her job to fetch new diapers and seal them with adhesive, or to protect the baby from falling leaves and twigs if you are walking outside. Praise the child profusely when she performs her duties successfully.

TEENAGER

OUT ALL NIGHT

Take the rest of the family out to breakfast so your teen comes home to an absolutely empty house. Spend the day having fun, shopping at the mall, going to an amusement park, watching movies. Come home late in the day and act like absolutely nothing happened. If they ask you where you were, snicker as if you have secret information.

BRINGS HOME "STUDY BUDDY"

Ask the pair what subject they plan to study. Express tremendous interest, saying that you always wanted to know more about it. Ask politely if they would mind if you sat in at the beginning, just to learn a bit. After you've established your presence in the room by asking a ton of questions, excuse yourself from their company. Return every half hour or so to seek clarification and ask additional questions.

ASKS TO BORROW CAR

Determine what car-dependent errands you can entrust to your teen and hand him a checklist of the errands (shopping list, dry-cleaning pickup, car wash or maintenance service) along with the keys. If he accepts, count yourself lucky and maintain a short list of errands always at the ready for when he next needs wheels. If he refuses, you will have succeeded in keeping the car safely at home.

Listens to Disturbing Music

Borrow a couple of CDs from your teen for your morning commute. Listen to the CDs, then come home and tell your child you like the bands and want to hear more from them. Talk about how you can relate to the lyrics. Learn a few bars and sing them off-key. Suggest that the two of you go to concerts together. Your teen will either change his musical tastes immediately or you'll have something in common to talk about.

Wears Disturbing Clothing

Emulate your teen's style of dress the next time you go out as a family. Tell her you think the look is "fly."

Chronic Oversleeper

Buy multiple, battery-powered alarm clocks, set them to the time you would like the teen to wake up (plus or minus a minute), and hide them in various places in the teen's room without her knowledge. Be sure that none are within reach of the bed. Call your teen's mobile phone. Bounce a tennis ball off her car to set off its alarm. Repeat for several weeks or as necessary until she has adapted to her early schedule.

IN-LAWS

Serve Terrible Dinner/Food

Develop a series of (fake) potent allergies to whatever it is they plan to cook. Alternatively, announce that you have a tremendously sensitive stomach and the only thing you can hold down is a bowl of cereal and/or a peanut butter sandwich. Eat before you arrive.

Criticize Career Choice

Ask the in-laws multiple, in-depth questions about their own careers. Become fascinated with their occupations, asking persistent sympathetic questions about the frustrations and real or potential downsides of their work. Express admiration for their abilities and perseverance, especially in the face of (point out a still more frustrating aspect of their profession). In doing so, you will have succeeded in distracting their criticism of you, expressing sympathy, and calling to mind painful doubts about their own careers all at once.

Not Good Enough for Son/Daughter

Alter your appearance for the worse bit by bit over a series of visits. Wear fake teeth, unflattering glasses, weight padding, wigs, blotchy or unexpected makeup. Cough frequently. After a few visits, arrive free of false afflictions and see much more they appreciate you.

JOINT VACATION

Get a separate bedroom, as far away from your in-laws' room as possible. Agree to spend *either* the day or the evening with them, while reserving the other half of the day as private time for you and your spouse. If your in-laws complain, tell them that with your careers and other obligations, you don't have enough time to spend with one another. When you are on your "alone" part of the day, go far away from the hotel.

POLITICAL DIFFERENCES

Become a student of history. Meticulously study the historical impact of your in-laws' political leanings. Elicit political discussions with your in-laws, making it abundantly clear that you not only understand their positions better than they do, but that you also can pull up insightful historical anecdotes to further prove your points. They will avoid political discussion when they see that arguing with you is no longer any fun.

CHAPTER 9

FOOD & COOKING

KITCHEN EMERGENCIES

HAND CUT WITH MEAT CLEAVER

Elevate the wound above your heart. Place direct pressure on the injury for 15 minutes. When the bleeding stops, dress the wound to prevent infection. Lacerations that are longer than ½ inch, are deep, or will not stop bleeding will likely require stitches.

OVEN ON FIRE

Keep oven door shut. Turn the oven off. Though smoke may pour out of the vents, ovens are designed to contain heat and flame, and the fire should burn out after several minutes. Do not open the oven door for at least 5 minutes, or until you are sure the fire is out, as you will only add oxygen to the fire. Keep your face back from the oven when you open the door. If the fire continues to burn for more than 10 minutes, call the fire department.

GREASE FIRE

Turn the range off. Put on large oven mitts (to the elbow, if available), pick up the lid to the pan/pot and carefully slide the lid over the pan to smother the fire. If the pan does not have a lid, smother the fire with a cookie sheet, coarse salt, or baking soda.

JAR WON'T OPEN

Rap on counter.

Pry lid with butterknife.

Hold under hot running water.

Use rubber band or towel
to improve grip.

Puncture lid to break seal.

**Try these techniques individually or together
to loosen a stuck jar lid.**

Gas Burner Won't Light

Lift the range cover and look underneath to determine if the pilot light on the line that feeds the burner is still lit. If not, and if there is no ambient smell of gas, light a long match and touch to pilot light line opening to relight. Never leave a burner in the "light" position while lighting the pilot light. Never light a match if you smell gas in the house. Open window and doors, then get out of the house and call the gas company.

Hands Smell Garlicky

Rub your hands across a stainless-steel utensil under running tap water.

Hot Pepper Oil on Hands

Create a solution of 10 parts water to 1 part household bleach. Soak your hands in the solution until the pain subsides. Always wear rubber gloves while handling hot peppers to avoid contact with capsaicin oil, most of which is located in the fibers that hold the seeds to the pepper flesh.

Teary While Cutting Onions

Put the onions in the freezer for 10 minutes before cutting. Remove and promptly chop or slice. Avoid cutting into the potent root of the onion, which contains the highest concentration of the tear-inducing sulfur.

Peer under the sink and press the reset button on the disposal unit. If the disposal still won't work, check the disposal motor for an Allen (hex) bolt in the housing and turn the bolt with an Allen wrench until the flywheel moves. If the clog remains, remove all items from the disposal and use the handle of a wooden spoon to move the impellers back and forth. Press the reset button. If the disposal is still clogged, use a purpose-specific disposal wrench to loosen the tension bolt and clear the jam.

COOKING CATASTROPHES

CAKE DOESN'T RISE

Cut the cake into thin slices, fry it in melted butter, then coat it with powdered sugar and serve.

CRACKED CHEESECAKE

Slice the cake in the kitchen before serving, or top with sliced berries or your favorite jam mixed with 1 tablespoon of liqueur to make it more spreadable. Allow the topping to seep into the crack, then add more topping to even the surface. To reduce cracks, place a pan of water on the oven rack below the cheesecake while it is baking.

OVERBEATEN EGG WHITES

Stir in 1 extra egg white for each 5 you have already beaten. Beat until the whites are of the texture required for the recipe. Remove about ¼ cup to correct for the extra white.

MEAT TOO DRY

Melt ½ stick of butter and mix with gravy or the pan drippings. Slice the meat thinly, place in a shallow baking dish, and smother with the mixture. Cover with foil and place in a 200°F oven for 10 minutes, then serve.

LOBSTERS ESCAPE

Close kitchen doors and cabinets to cut off escape routes. Wear oven mitts to protect you from the lobsters' pincers. Use a pot lid to herd the lobsters. Grasp each by the body from behind and place in a large, lidded pot of water, claws first.

Lumpy Gravy

Pour the gravy through a mesh strainer. To avoid lumps, combine the thickening agent (flour, cornstarch, arrowroot) with enough liquid to make a paste, then whisk the paste into the hot liquid to evenly distribute it.

Soup Too Salty

Add 2 raw, chopped potatoes to the soup, cook for 10 to 15 minutes, then remove. Honey can also help even out a salty taste, or adding more of the other ingredients. To avoid oversalting the soup, season it just before serving.

Sauce Too Thick

Whisk in broth (chicken, beef, or vegetable) until the sauce reaches the desired thickness, or pour the sauce through a strainer.

Sauce Too Thin

Add 1 to 2 tablespoons of cornstarch to some water. Create a paste, then whisk it into the sauce. Adding dry cornstarch directly to the sauce will create lumps. If you are making a tomato-based sauce, add 1 to 2 tablespoons of concentrated tomato paste and stir to evenly distribute.

Sauce Too Garlicky

Remove any visible garlic pieces using a slotted spoon or handheld strainer, then add honey to balance the flavor.

Brown Sugar Is Hardened

Place hard brown sugar in a microwave-proof dish and cover with a couple of damp paper towels. Microwave for 30 seconds to 1 minute, then check to see if the sugar has softened, carefully removing and setting aside partially loosened sugar with a fork and re-microwaving still-hard clumps. Repeat as necessary, watching closely to make sure the sugar does not melt.

Wilted Lettuce

Fill your sink with warm water. Submerge the lettuce for 5 to 10 minutes, then remove from the water. Dry the lettuce with a salad spinner or paper towels, cover the lettuce with a damp towel, and refrigerate for at least 30 minutes.

Soufflé Collapses

Cover the top with whipped cream or a very thin layer of chocolate pudding, and serve "baked pudding." To prevent a soufflé from collapsing, use room-temperature beaten eggs, never open the oven door while the soufflé is baking, and place the soufflé on the lower oven rack to give it room to expand.

OUT OF INGREDIENT

Ingredient	Amount Called for	Substitution
Baking powder	1 teaspoon	¼ teaspoon baking soda plus ⅝ teaspoon cream of tartar
Butter, solid	1 cup	1 cup margarine or 1 cup vegetable shortening for baking
Butter, melted		Equal portion of oil
Buttermilk	1 cup	1 tablespoon lemon juice or vinegar plus enough regular milk to make 1 cup (allow to stand 5 minutes)
Cocoa powder	¼ cup	1 ounce unsweetened chocolate (decrease fat in recipe by 1½ teaspoons)
Cornstarch	1 tablespoon	2 tablespoons all-purpose flour
Cream, half and half	1 cup	⅞ cup whole milk plus ½ tablespoon butter or margarine
Cream, heavy (40% fat)	1 cup	¾ cup milk plus ⅓ cup butter or margarine (for use in cooking and baking)
Cream of tartar	½ teaspoon	1½ teaspoons lemon juice or vinegar
Garlic	1 clove	⅛ teaspoon garlic powder
Honey	1 cup	1¼ cups sugar plus ¼ cup additional liquid called for in recipe
Lemon juice, fresh	1 teaspoon	½ teaspoon vinegar
Mayonnaise	1 cup	1 cup yogurt or 1 cup sour cream
Molasses	1 cup	¾ cup sugar plus 1¼ teaspoons cream of tartar (increase liquid in recipe by 5 tablespoons)
Shortening, for baking	1 cup	1⅛ cups butter or margarine (decrease salt called for in recipe by ½ teaspoon)
Sugar, brown	1 cup, firmly packed	1 cup granulated sugar
Sugar, confectioners'	1 cup	½ cup plus 1 tablespoon granulated sugar
Sugar, granulated	1 cup	1¾ cups confectioners' sugar or 1 cup packed light brown sugar
Vinegar	1 teaspoon	2 teaspoons lemon juice
Yogurt	1 cup	1 cup milk plus 1 tablespoon lemon juice

MESSES

DISHWASHER FLOODS KITCHEN

Turn the dishwasher off, or close the valve on the water pipe that feeds it. Run the garbage disposal in the sink to eliminate any food items that may have caused a backup. Mop water from the floor. Empty the dishwasher, then run again on the rinse cycle to remove standing water. If flooding recurs, call for service.

SPILLED OIL

Pour coarse salt on the oil, allow it to sit for several minutes, then wipe it up. Granulated table salt will also work, though it is slightly less effective, as will flour. After wiping, clean remaining oil with a bit of dish detergent and a paper towel. Do not use soap and water, which will only spread the spill.

SPAGHETTI SAUCE ON WHITE TABLECLOTH

Scrape food particles from the tablecloth with the edge of a spoon. Mix 1 teaspoon of a mild, nonbleaching clothing detergent with 1 cup of warm water, apply, and blot the stain with a paper towel. If the stain remains, mix 1 tablespoon of household ammonia with ½ cup of cold water, then blot the stain. If the stain continues to hold, repeat blotting with the detergent/water mixture, then blot with a clean, wet sponge.

WINE & SPIRITS

Wine Is "Corked"

Throw it away—there is nothing that can be done to fix the wine. A "corked" wine has been spoiled by a cork contaminated by trichloranisole, or TCA, which gives the wine a musty smell and an off taste.

Uncorking Wine without Corkscrew

Place the handle-end of a narrow wooden serving spoon on top of the cork. Using firm, steady pressure, push the cork into the bottle. If the cork won't budge, tap a hammer or meat tenderizer on the spoon to push it through.

Opening Beer Bottle without Bottle Opener

Unfasten your belt buckle and move the "tooth" of the buckle to one side. Fit the cap into the buckle so that one edge is wedged against the buckle and pry off the cap.

Champagne Headache

Take an over-the-counter pain reliever, drink plenty of water, take a walk in fresh air, and be patient. Avoid coffee, which can be harsh on an already unsettled stomach. To reduce the likelihood of a hangover, eat while drinking (especially high-fat foods), and drink a glass of water or juice between glasses of bubbly.

WINE HAS SEDIMENT

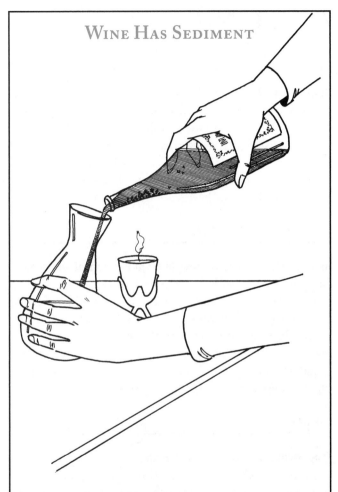

Let wine settle upright for 24 hours. Remove the cork and foil to expose the bottleneck. Pour the wine from the bottle to the decanter by candlelight. Stop pouring the wine as soon as sediment approaches the neck and discard the bottle's remaining contents.

GRILLING

Beer-Can Chicken Explosion

Remove chicken from the grill with long barbecue tongs and place on a platter. Once the can has detonated, the chicken poses no further explosive danger. Once the chicken has cooled, discard, as aluminum shrapnel from the can may have embedded itself in the chicken. Always open the beer can and take several big gulps before putting inside chicken. Pre-grease the can for easy removal.

Kabob Skewer Wound

Remove the food or marinade from the end of the skewer and pull the skewer from your body with one quick, firm tug. Irrigate the wound with a stream of cold water for 5 minutes; a small puncture wound should not bleed profusely. Carefully examine the wound. If any foreign material is lodged in the wound, seek medical attention. If the wound appears clean, apply pressure to stop bleeding, then wash with soap and warm water and bandage.

Apron on Fire

Stop, drop, and roll to smother the flames. For a smoldering apron, quickly remove and throw to the ground, away from any gas tank supplying the fuel for the grill or dry leaves in the yard. Stomp the apron wearing closed-toed shoes, or douse with water, beer, or soda. Do not stomp if you are barefoot or are wearing sandals or flip-flops.

CHARRED MEAT

Remove the meat from the grill. Using a very sharp knife, cut ⅛ inch from the charred side(s), then return the meat to the grill if the interior is below 160°F. If the meat is overcooked, add melted butter to prepared barbecue sauce and smother the meat with the sauce. If the meat is extremely dry and overcooked, chop it finely and mix it with the sauce; serve on a bun or over rice or potatoes.

BARBECUE SAUCE IN EYE

Use a clean turkey baster to flush the eye continuously with cool water until the pain subsides.

GREASE FIRE

Smother the fire with coarse salt. Immediately cover the grill, and make sure all vents are closed. Wait 30 seconds, then uncover slowly, holding lid at arm's length and watching for flare-ups. To reduce the chance of grease drippings catching fire, pile coals on one side of the grill and cook the food on the other.

GRILL TIPS OVER

Right the grill, then pick up hot coals using tongs and return them to grill. Soak the ground in the area of the tipover plus several feet with water from a hose.

FISH FLAKING APART

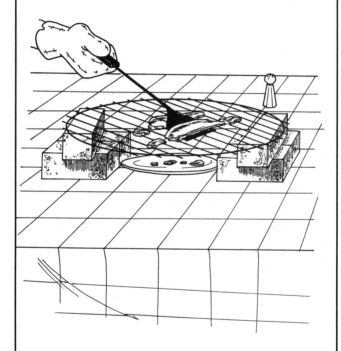

Remove the metal grill from the flame using barbecue mitts.
Place the grill between two stacks of two bricks, with the fish over an
open center area. Place a pan under the grill/fish to catch flaking
pieces, then remove remaining fish with a spatula coated in olive oil or
butter. Garnish with lemon and serve as fish hash.

DINNER PARTIES

UNEXPECTED GUEST

Act delighted. Add another place setting and chair to the table. If the chair is mismatched, sit on it yourself so the new guest does not feel out of place. If you are serving individual capons or steaks and are one short, divide portions in the kitchen out of sight of the guests and serve precut, or share a single portion with your co-host. Serve extra bread or salad to help rebalance portions.

UNEXPECTED VEGETARIAN OR VEGAN

Invite the vegan into the kitchen and take inventory of the fridge and cabinets. Assemble any available food items free of animal products to create a cocktail party platter-like spread, including fresh sliced fruits and vegetables; mixed nuts; chips, bread, or crackers (free of lard or animal proteins) topped with salsa, peanut butter, or hummus. Vegans are generally accustomed to spending extra time gathering food, and often enjoy being resourceful.

FOOD TAKES LONGER TO COOK THAN PLANNED

Serve more cocktails. Delay appetizers or serve in courses. Serve salad as a separate course, followed by a "palate cleanser" of sorbet, cheese, fruit, or anything else you might have sufficiently onhand. Discreetly cover clocks with dishtowels or leafy potted plants.

Oyster Aphrodisiac Overdose

Eat plenty of garlic and onions to protect yourself from unwanted advances. Encourage the oyster eater to talk about baseball, taxes, or real estate.

Conversation Gets Heated

Disrupt the conversational flow by serving the next round of food, dessert, coffee, or another round of drinks. Tap the side of your glass with a fork and offer a toast to family, friendship, or togetherness. Solicit help from your dinner companions for some complicated, fictitious problem that can become the all-consuming focus of attention.

Inappropriate Toast

Drop or knock to the floor a utensil or unbreakable item and pretend to bump your head while retrieving it (rap the table with your hand), or feign a coughing fit. When your dinner companions ask if you are okay, hesitate to further distract attention from the thwarted toast, then say "Yes, I think so. Thank you. Let's just eat."

Post-Turkey Tryptophan Coma

Drink caffeinated beverages (cola, coffee, tea) and eat sweets (ice cream, fruit) to help you stay awake. If you cannot keep your eyes open, take a walk outside in the fresh air, which will help to revive you.

Seated Next to a Boor

Turn the conversation into a game. Allow yourself to take another sip of wine each time the boor says something offensive or clueless, or keep a running tally of each time he tells a story about himself. Try to ensnare other diners into the conversation by offering details from the boor's tale for comment ("Matt, you've got a lawnmower, don't you?"). Excuse yourself from the table—to the kitchen, restroom, or to get something from your car—and remain away from the table for as long as possible until the boor turns to another conversational victim.

Ejecting Bone/Gristle

Cover your hand with your napkin, bringing it to your mouth with a dabbing motion, and discreetly push the gristle into the napkin with your tongue. Do not spit, which will be audible. Excuse yourself and empty the napkin in the trash (if cloth) or throw it away (if paper), or replace on your lap but leave folded so gristle will not fall out. At the end of the meal, empty napkin contents onto plate and cover with napkin.

RESTAURANTS

Lost/Canceled Reservation

Maintain your composure. Calmly and politely tell the host the day and time you called to make the reservation, and the name of the person you spoke to. Express disappointment, saying that this is your favorite restaurant and you'd made the reservation to celebrate your promotion/anniversary/birthday/release from prison. If the restaurant cannot accommodate you, ask the host to get you a table at another restaurant nearby.

Seated at Worst Table

Have a drink at the bar. Ask the maitre d' if you can give the table to the next waiting guest and wait for the next available table, or ask that your table be moved to a more suitable location.

Birthday Party at Next Table

Ask that your entrées be served when the birthday party is finishing their dessert if it is impossible for you to be reseated elsewhere in the restaurant. Sing along loudly when the cake is served, then ask that you also be served a piece.

Can't Pronounce Menu Items

Describe the item you wish to eat by noun only: You'll have the fish, the beef, the chicken, the ravioli, the merlot, or the special. Point to the line item on the menu to aid in identification and help distinguish between multiple preparations. Alternatively, wait for your dining companions to order, or point to food served at another table, and say "I'll have what she's having."

Candle on Table Lights Menu on Fire

Drop the menu onto the tabletop and knock over glasses of water, wine, and beer until flames are extinguished. If you haven't yet been served any drinks, cover the flaming menu with an upside down dinner plate and press to cut off oxygen and extinguish the flames. Announce to the other patrons not to order the "menu flambé."

Rude/Absent Waiter

Leave the restaurant if you have not ordered your meal. If you have already ordered, ask to speak to the manager and explain the situation. He or she should address the waiter immediately and resolve the conflict. If the situation is not resolved to your satisfaction, do not leave a tip. If the service charge is included in your tab, pay with a credit card and dispute the service charge with the card issuer.

CHAPTER 10

STAGES OF LIFE

KID

Dodgeball in Stomach

Curl your body inward with the impact of the ball. Stretch your arms outward, fingertips almost touching, to encircle the ball and try to catch it as it rebounds off your body—which will force your opponent out of the game.

Fell off Monkeybars

Cover your head and neck with your arms and try to guide your fall away from the bars and onto the playground's rubber padding, sand, or woodchips. Test movement of your arms and legs to be sure there is no sharp pain before getting up. If you have to cry, do so only to get the attention of a nearby adult who may assist you.

Blatantly Excluded from Game

Walk away from the competition. Do not hang around, watch, or play near the game, as it will only make you look pathetic and prompt abuse from the participants. Channel your feelings of insult and anger toward self-improvement, practicing the game at home with your family and on your own. The better you get, the more ready you'll be to contribute to a team when you have the chance.

Unbutton your shirt or coat, starting with the top button, just enough to slip out of your garment and slide to the ground. Then unhook your clothes and put them back on. If you were hung by your coat, you just leave it there on the hook.

Live in the moment by concentrating only on those things immediately around you. Don't get overwhelmed by grief by thinking of the things you miss from home. Pretend that you have been exiled to a foreign country or distant planet; take note of the strange new smells, sounds, terrain, food, and behavior of the locals so you can report back on them when you return home from your adventure.

WET PANTS

Hold a book, bookbag, or large toy in front of the affected area to cover it and move toward a liquid dispenser such as a drinking fountain, faucet, soda machine, or full standing container. Spill more liquid on yourself to mask the wet spot and make it larger, dribbling the liquid down the front of your shirt and pants. Publicly bemoan your own clumsiness and ask to be sent home to change clothes.

SIBLING BLAMES YOU

Accept full responsibility for whatever you are being accused of. Grant that the sibling is right on every count and that you are truly sorry. Later, as your stunned parents try to decide your punishment, pull them aside and calmly explain that you had nothing whatever to do with the incident and simply acted to avoid a loud, messy conflict. Suggest that your sibling's troublemaking behavior might be a desperate cry for parental attention.

Grounded

Make the most of being stuck at home by learning important life skills that will help you down the road. For example, learn how to make a proper omelet (hint: the pan must be sizzling hot in order to cook the eggs as fast as possible) or how to maintain your balance in high heels, if appropriate.

Bad Report Card

Appear to be brooding, with a lot on your mind, on the day you bring the report card home. When confronted by your parents, show them the poor grades, profess deep disappointment in yourself, and offer to accept any punishment that will not cut into your study time. Spend a generous amount of time over the next few days locked in your room with books and papers spread out all around you on your bed. Only relent after your parents beg you to take it easy once in a while and enjoy being a kid.

Bully Picks a Fight

Ferociously attack the moment the bully's attention is directed toward you, without giving him any time to prepare. Savagely flail your arms and legs, landing as many blows in a short, controlled burst as possible, all the while screaming at the top of your lungs. You might well get flattened, but in the future the bully will look for an easier, more docile target than what you've become.

Teacher Always Calls on You in Class

Develop a fake stutter and speak with long, awkward pauses between words so that the teacher is forced to help you finish your sentences. If she catches you speaking normally outside of class, explain that you only have difficulty when you are put on the spot in front of large groups of your peers.

Bad Lunch

Offer to trade the offending lunch items for food from classmates' lunches. Even if the trade does not yield an item you yourself wish to eat, the item might yet be traded again to another classmate for something you *do* want to eat. Try offering lunch "futures"—trading items to be eaten today for food you can bring in at a later date.

TEENAGER

FRIEND COPIES YOUR STYLE/LOOK

Perform a reverse retail fakeout. A friend who bites your style is likely to try to do so again. Offer to go shopping together, express interest in a tragic new style that you actually have no intention of ever wearing, regretting that you can't afford the new look just yet. Cite evidence from TV or in magazines of fools sporting the look and wait for the friend to take the bait.

FRIEND STEALS BOYFRIEND/GIRLFRIEND

Hint that your former flame had a recurring STD, so it's just as well that you are no longer an item. In the meantime, find someone your former friend had a thing for and do everything in your power to make him fall for you.

MEETING DATE'S PARENTS

Make direct eye contact. Speak clearly and refer to them as "Mr." and "Mrs." unless they ask you to do otherwise. Do not perform any complicated handshake unless initiated by the parent—a brief, firm shake with direct eye contact is sufficient—and do not hug or kiss parents unless they make the first move. Keep a distance of 3 feet. Turn off your mobile phone or pager before the introduction. Pet the family dog or cat. Let your date determine the exit strategy beforehand and follow her lead.

CAUGHT PASSING A NOTE IN CLASS

Swallow the note immediately. Do not give the teacher a chance to grab it and read it out loud. You are already in trouble for passing a note—there is no point in adding the humiliation of having it read to the class.

Controlling Parents

Cite greater independence granted to brothers, sisters, cousins, friends, and other kids in the neighborhood, on television, in movies, and literature as examples of the right and just state of personal freedom. Cut deals for incremental increases in independence in order to build trust. Ask for a one-time curfew extension of 15 or 20 minutes and come home within the limit before later asking to stay out an extra hour. Take it in small steps and they won't realize how far you've gotten until your new liberty has become the norm.

Embarrassing Parents

Limit the amount of time that you are publicly associated with your parents. Concede family time at a dimly lit, out-of-the-way restaurant your friends would never visit. When walking together in public, keep a few steps ahead of or behind your parents. If classmates are approaching, duck into a nearby shop. Exit after friends have passed.

No Driver's License

Explain that you'd rather not drive. Say that learning to drive is a waste of time since you will soon be moving to a big city with great public transportation. Explain that you are just doing your part for the environment, as it's better to walk, bike, and carpool. Meanwhile, do favors for or outright bribe multiple friends with drivers' licenses to be sure you have wheels whenever you need a lift.

Start a conga line. After that's finished, you should be flushed and sweaty as if you'd really been dancing for a while and you can take your seat without looking like you're being aloof.

Mono

Gargle with a warm saltwater solution 5 times each day to relieve your sore throat, and take ibuprofen or acetaminophen for achiness and fever. Avoid strenuous exercise, lifting heavy objects, or contact sports; get a lot of bed rest, especially when first diagnosed; and drink plenty of fluids. Do not share a glass, kiss, or otherwise share your saliva with anyone until you have fully recovered, possibly in 2 to 3 months. Symptoms of mononucleosis include sore throat, achiness, fever, fatigue, sensitivity to light, enlarged spleen and liver, and swollen glands in the neck, armpit, and groin. If you have mono and you feel a severe, sharp pain on the left side of your upper abdomen, seek emergency medical care immediately, as your spleen may have ruptured.

Stuck in Locker

Peer through the air vents and wait for a teacher to walk past, then knock and kick the door to get his attention. Ask him to fetch the janitor to open the lock. To entertain yourself as you wait, yell "Boo!" each time a student passes to see how many people you can freak out.

SINGLE LIFE

HOT TUB RASH

Use an over-the-counter anti-itching ointment such as hydrocortisone. Allow the rash to breathe and dry up; do not seal it with a dressing. Do not go back into a public hot tub or pool—or share clothes or towels—until the rash has healed and disappeared, as you will remain contagious until it goes away. Always shower with soap after hot-tubbing.

TICKLISH WHEN MAKING OUT

Slow your movements and maintain solid rather than brushing contact so that your partner will mimic your approach. Move your partner's hands to her sides or lap.

SWEATY PALMS

Spread talcum powder or cornstarch over your palms before going out. Bring along two folded-up handkerchiefs with additional powder, keeping one in each jacket or pants pocket. When you feel your hands dampen, put them in your pockets and grab hold of the hankies with a quick, fist-clenching motion, as if you're searching for loose change or your keys. If the problem persists, use a special, unscented palm-and-heel antiperspirant.

CAUGHT IN MOSH PIT AT CONCERT

Go limp if you have been hoisted aloft. Keep your arms out-stretched. You will likely be deposited on your feet once the song or set ends. If standing in the pit, keep your arms in front of your chest, bent slightly, palms out, to give yourself a breathing cushion.

Date Stands You Up

Remain upbeat and confident, bantering in a humorously self-effacing manner with the bartenders and/or waitstaff. If you are in a bar, take a seat at the counter and chat with fellow patrons. If you are at a restaurant, look to see if there are any other single diners who seem interesting to you. If so, casually approach them and ask if they would enjoy some company.

Date Won't Stop Talking about Ex

If you still consider the date a prospective partner, announce that from now on, you will respond to any mention of the ex with a statement about a subject that does not interest her (e.g.: "I really never felt like Bob could open up around me." "When you add an air-ram to a '68 Charger you can make 25 more horsepower, but you have to swap the exhaust or you'll blow a seal"). If you no longer consider the date a prospect, say that your cellphone just rang in vibrate mode and "take a call" from your brother/sister/cousin, whose boy-/girlfriend has just walked out. Explain that you are urgently needed elsewhere.

Date Leaves with Someone Else

Revel in the fact that you have just been spared anywhere from 3 to 12 months of heartbreak, regret, and self-loathing. Approach sympathetic-looking singles in your vicinity to make the best of the situation.

DATE ALWAYS EXPECTS YOU TO PAY

Make reservations at a fine restaurant, let your date order whatever he would like, and then order the smallest, most inexpensive appetizer you can find on the menu for yourself. If your date asks you why you made such a small order, explain that you want him to enjoy a fine meal, but that you can only afford to pay for one dinner. If your date relents and offers to pay his half, order your entrée and enjoy the rest of your experience; if your date doesn't try to make amends, tell him you have to go to the bathroom, leave the premises, and don't look back.

DATE WEARING TOO MUCH PERFUME/COLOGNE

Dampen a cloth or napkin and tell your date she has a little dirt on her neck. Use the napkin to wipe as much of the offending perfume/cologne as possible. If the strong scent remains, or if the odor is coming from the wrist area, try to take the date somewhere frigid, like a chilly movie theater or a slow walk outdoors at night. Perfume is intensified by heat, so making the body colder will help to reduce the power of the fragrance.

MARRIED LIFE

Forgot Anniversary

Buy last-minute tickets to a tropical isle for the weekend.
Make it seem as if your "forgetting" was only a setup so
you could spring this wonderful surprise on your spouse
when you hand over the tickets. Note that this will only
work once. Bite your lip, pay off your credit card, and etch
the date of your anniversary forever in your mind. Consider a tattoo.

Lacking in Romance

Surprise your mate with unexpected behavior—a passion-
ate good-bye kiss instead of a perfunctory peck; dinner by
candlelight; a bubble bath for two. Ask how your partner
would rate your "love life" on a scale of 1 to 10—the mere
fact of having the conversation should make your level of
mutual satisfaction increase. If the pressure of romance is
too great, agree to take turns initiating "intimacy."

Nothing to Say at the Dinner Table

**Tell your partner that you want to "talk about something
different."** Ask open-ended, thought-provoking questions
to elicit more interesting responses. Examples of such
questions include: If you could spend a day with a
celebrity, who would it be? What was your favorite childhood toy? What vegetable do you most resemble? Use
your imagination and knowledge of one another.

BUYING A HOUSE TOGETHER

Make separate lists of the features your ideal home would have before you start looking. Include basics such as "new construction" or "older home," "near grocery store" or "near corner bar," "in good school district" or "swinging, childfree neighborhood," "close to my parents" or "as far away from his parents as possible." See where your lists overlap to determine what's important to both of you.

SURVIVING PREGNANCY

Use the BABY mnemonic: BE patient—crying jags and emotional breakdowns are not uncommon during pregnancy for women or men. ASK often—"Is there anything you need?" "Can I massage your feet?" but not "Are you nuts?" or "Why are we doing this?" BECOME educated—for every book about pregnancy you read, read one about parenting to prepare for what's coming next. YOU matter, too—find the new balance that allows you all to remain individuals and still be a family.

CAUGHT BY KIDS "ENTRE ACT"

Shriek and cover yourselves completely with a bedsheet. If you have not frightened the children away, explain to them that they startled mommy and daddy and that good little boys and girls always knock before entering a room. If asked what you were doing, explain that such acts are only permitted between mommies and daddies, birds, and bees who love each other very much.

Winning an Argument

Agree with whatever your partner is saying wholeheartedly, and agree that your more reasonable position is wrong. Later, when his guard is relaxed, ask innocent-seeming questions for clarification, allowing him to undermine his ridiculous stance with further clarifications, until it is plainly obvious that your take is the right one. Do your best to make it seem as if he came to this conclusion himself, then agree with him.

Spouse Snores

Lift the nearest side of your spouse's pillow until she turns onto her side. Alternately, flop around forcefully on your side until her sleep is disturbed and she turns over. Nudge with your elbow or a soft kick if more subtle methods do not yield results. Wear earplugs or noise canceling earphones if you are comfortable sleeping on your back. Encourage her to refrain from alcohol (which deepens snoring) and drink caffeine (which reduces snoring) before turning in for the night.

Spouse Crowds You out of Bed

Be the first to get into bed and stake out more than your usual turf by lying in the middle of the bed so that your partner occupies the space you leave available. Once he goes to sleep, move to your usual sleeping position and spot and place pillows between you in the open space to resist encroachment later in the night.

MIDDLE AGE

Midlife Crisis

Determine the nature of your distress. It is natural to feel some discontent with your life and question its meaning when you near the age of 40. Common triggers of existential anguish are financial troubles, death of a parent, feeling older, dealing with teenage children, impending retirement, and the "empty nest" syndrome. If you are near the age of 40 and want to leave your spouse or your job, buy an inappropriate car, or wear clothes marketed toward 20-year-olds, you are probably having a midlife crisis. Put off making life decisions until you regain your sense of balance.

Adjusting to Bifocals

Wear the lenses all the time for the first few weeks, even though you may not need them for everything you do. Look down only with your eyes—without moving your head—when reading, holding the reading material closer to your body so that you are looking through the lowest part of the lenses. To help your optometrist determine the placement of your corrective lenses, tell the doctor about the types of activities you participate in that require clear vision. Improperly placed lenses can cause accidents while walking, climbing stairs, and while driving.

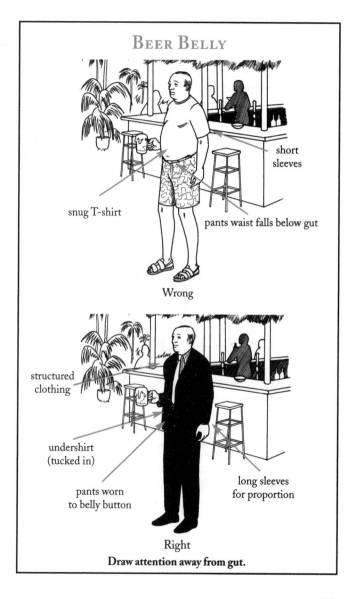

BEER BELLY

short sleeves

snug T-shirt

pants waist falls below gut

Wrong

structured clothing

undershirt (tucked in)

pants worn to belly button

long sleeves for proportion

Right

Draw attention away from gut.

Hot Flashes

Avoid spicy foods and caffeine-laced drinks, which are common triggers for hot flashes. Keeping your weight down and exercising regularly can also help prevent hot flashes. Dress in layers to help manage your temperature, drink ice water, and keep the A/C on in your house, especially at night to help reduce night sweats. Put all your bulky sweaters and fleece garments into storage and celebrate the idea that your hands and feet won't be cold again for a while.

Going Bald

Reduce stress, maintain a healthful high-protein diet, and take multivitamins—temporary hair loss may sometimes result from illness, tension, or poor nutrition. For women, partial hair loss sometimes occurs after pregnancy or going off birth control pills, and more permanent hair loss after menopause. Perms, coloring, wigs, shawls, and hats can help mask symptoms. For men, shave entire head in advance of notable male pattern baldness.

Going Gray

Get the hippest, most avant-garde hair cut of your life. Do not dye your hair. Take on an air of sophistication by wearing fashionable black ensembles with dark capes and dark-rimmed glasses and laughing vigorously while drinking elegant flutes of dark wine in public.

Seven-Year Itch

Take comfort in the cliché of the situation: Recognize that it's normal for couples who are together this long to weather rough patches, and that feelings of discontent or restlessness are also normal when people perceive themselves in static long-term situations. Change a few routines. Pursue new hobbies and interests to make yourself more interesting, to yourself and to your spouse, and share them with one another.

Handling Being Called "Sir" or "Ma'am"

Preemptively refer to everyone by "sir" or "ma'am" first, before they say it to you. You will appear to have impeccable manners, even as your excessive courtesy unsettles younger service-industry workers.

SENIOR CITIZEN

SHRINKING IN STATURE

Buy shoe lifts or sturdy, wide-heel platform shoes or boots. Style your hair upward and wear shirts, sweaters, and coats that are slightly too small for you, allowing your wrists to show more than usual. Vertical striped clothing can also add the illusion of height. Lift weights and exercise regularly to gain some muscle mass to make up for the lost size.

HAIRY EARS

Trim hair with an electric shaver or nose and ear hair trimmer with rotary blades. Do not use scissors, which risk puncture injury, and avoid using fixed-blade razors, which are more likely to scrape the sensitive skin at the edge of the ear.

FORGOT GRANDCHILDREN'S NAMES

Wait for the children to refer to themselves and take note of the names they use. Give the children nicknames, such as "Dusty" or "Blondie"—try to make them memorable, perhaps based on a physical trait, so you can use the nicknames in the future. In a real jam, "Kiddo" is a good catch-all for any grandchild. Avoid nicknames that might be considered cruel, such as "Tubby" or "Jughead."

Dentures Won't Stay in Place

Get the dentures refitted with a new lining. If you have to use a fixative, start with a minimum amount of adhesive around the perimeter of your denture. Gradually work up from there until you find a comfort zone.

Age Spots

Apply an alpha hydroxy acid gel to reduce the coloring. Wear hats and long-sleeve shirts when outdoors, and use a liberal amount of high-SPF sun block daily on your face and hands to protect your skin from further damage. Age spots have more to do with the sun—skin pigment buildup from previous tanning—than with age, and are benign. Because some melanomas resemble them, have your doctor look at them during your annual checkup.

Hearing-Aid Feedback

Make sure the hearing aid is properly inserted. Check the volume, as it may be turned too high. Remove scarves or hats covering the aid; sound can bounce off these garments and cause feedback. Feedback can also occur if the hearing aid no longer fits to the ear; over time, the shape of the ear can change, causing the aid to become loose. Call your audiologist for refitting.

OUT-OF-CONTROL MOTOR HOME

Steer into a skid. Apply even brake pressure and shift into second or third gear to help slow the motor home. If possible, use an incline in the road to help naturally slow the vehicle even further; pull to the side of the road with your hazard lights on, and slowly pull up on the emergency brake, continuing to apply regular brake pressure, until you come to a complete stop.

Controlling Hyperactive Grandchildren

Have a breath-holding contest. Encourage the children to take slow, deep breaths—in through the nose and out through the mouth—as they prepare for the contest. Have them do this for several minutes. Dim the lights or close the curtains. Run your hand through their hair or give them a light massage on the shoulders as they are practicing their breathing. If they are still hyper after the contest, take them outside and hold a sprinting contest until you've worn them out.

Filling Time During Retirement

Rediscover your childhood hobbies. If you liked playing baseball, start following your local team and keeping an official scorecard. If you always wanted to be an astronaut, buy a good telescope and track the configurations and movement of the stars and planets. Discover new, ongoing activities that can be creatively or emotionally rewarding, such as gardening, artistic activities, or volunteer work.

Getting Your Kids to Take You In

Prove to your kids that you will remain independent and autonomous. Offer to cook meals, babysit, help clean, and do laundry when you're around; travel as much as possible to stay out of their hair. Suggest gently that you aren't looking for a place to spend the rest of your years, but a home base for when you're between exotic trips.

Choose a place you find comfortably challenging, either physically or mentally, to keep yourself spry. Spend time at each prospective residence, talking to the residents, to get a real sense of how it operates and what the general vibe is. Ask if you can spend a night there to see how things really work. Avoid any place whose primary "recreation" is the TV lounge.

PLANNING YOUR FUNERAL

Shop around. Think about what you've liked and disliked at funerals you've attended. Make a list of the things that are important to you. Do you want to be buried or cremated? Do you want music played? Are there any specific words or poems you want read? Then record your decisions for your family. You are the only one who knows if you have a preference between the tiki or cherry caskets; express yourself now, while you still can.

SELECTED RESOURCES

African Wildlife Foundation
American Academy of Allergy, Asthma, and Immunology, National
    Allergy Bureau
American Academy of Otolaryngology—Head and Neck Surgery
American Heart Association
American Optometric Association
American Osteopathic College of Dermatology
American Society for the Prevention of Cruelty to Animals
American Society of Plastic Surgeons
Animal Management Inc.
Animals of Africa by Thomas B. Allen
Armed Forces Pest Management Board
AskDrSears.com
Audiology Awareness Campaign
Beaufort County Public Library, Beaufort, South Carolina
Berry Bros. & Rudd Ltd.
British Coatings Federation
The British Horological Institute
British United Provident Association (BUPA)
California Tan
Canadian Council on Animal Care
The Cat Owner's Manual by Sam Stall and Dr. David Brunner
Certified Horsemanship Association
CoolNurse.com
Cornell University Department of Crop and Soil Sciences
Centers for Disease Control and Prevention
Delaware Division of Public Health
Diabetes Services, Inc.
The Dog Owner's Manual by Sam Stall and Dr. David Brunner
DoItYourself.com
Eco Living Center
eMedicine.com

Epicurious.com
FDA Consumer magazine
Ferret News
Fodors.com
Genie of Fairview Door Co.
GlobalGourmet.com
GlobalSecurity.org
Good Housekeeping Heloise Household Helpline
Outwitting Poison Ivy by Susan Carol Hauser
HealthTouch.com
The Heimlich Institute
Hermit-crabs.com
How to Behave by Caroline Tiger
Illinois Department of Public Health
Iowa State University Extension Answer Line
LlamaWeb.com
Massachusetts General Hospital Burns Service
The Mayo Clinic
McMaster University Campus Health Centre
Medical College of Wisconsin HealthLink
Medicine.net
Merck.com
Michigan State University Panda Habitat Research in China
Modern Ferret magazine
National Ag Safety Database
National Institute of Arthritis and Musculoskeletal and Skin Diseases
The National Institute of Neurological Disorders and Stroke
National Institutes of Health: United States National
    Library of Medicine
National Pollen and Aerobiology Research Unit, Institute of Health
    and Social Care, University of Worcester, England
National Safety Council
Nemours Foundation
Newport Beach Fire Department Community Emergency Response
    Team, Newport Beach, California

North Dakota State University Extension Service
OhioHealth
Ontario Dental Association
Palo Alto Medical Foundation
Pawprints and Purrs, Inc.
PetEducation.com
Prevention.com
PopularMechanics.com
Portland Parks & Recreation, City of Portland, Oregon
PsychologyToday.com
Save the Rhino International
Silverado Vineyards
South Florida Ferret Help Line
State of Pennsylvania Department of Environmental Protection,
      Bureau of Deep Mine Safety
Steven Tamaccio, owner of Estetica Salons, Philadelphia
Terminix Inc.
Texas A&M University System Aggie Horticulture Network
TheCarConnection.com
ThisOldHouse.com
Toronto Medical Laboratories and Mount Sinai Hospital
      Department of Microbiology
U.S. Consumer Product Safety Commission
U.S. Food and Drug Administration
U.S. Environmental Protection Agency
The University of Illinois at Urbana-Champaign
      McKinley Health Center
The University of Michigan Kellogg Eye Center
The University of North Carolina Highway Safety Research Center
University of Pittsburgh Medical Center
WebMD.com
WildlifeSafari.info
WomansDay.com

INDEX

A

abdominal cramp, 30
actors/celebrities, 165–66
agent won't return calls, 166
age spots, 281
agoraphobia attack, 21
ailments, 27–36
air conditioning blows out in
    hot weather, 84
air travel, 209–210
alcoholic beverages, 248–49
algae in fish tank, 113
allergies
    cats, 109
    hay fever, 36
amnesia, 33
amusement parks, 215–216
animal-proofing camp site, 204
ankle, sprained, 25, 191
anniversary, forgotten, 273
antifreeze, drunk by cat, 106
appetite, lost, 29
apron on fire, 250
aquariums, cracked, 111
arguments, winning, 275
arm
    broken, 26
    caught under boulder, 191
    stuck in bus door, 211
artery, spurting, 37
artwork, crooked, 75
athlete's foot, 56
avalanches, 146
award acceptance speech,
    forgotten, 165

B

babies, 177, 228–29
bald, going, 278
ball boys, injured, 138
barbecue
    sauce in eye, 251
    singes hair, 42
    See also grilling
barbell, trapped under, 64
bar fights, 174
barking at night, 102
bar, overcrowded, 176
bartenders, 174–76
baseball, 130–31
basement, flooded, 79
basketball, 127–29
bath, child won't take, 232
bats living in garage, 93
beaches, 194–97
bears, 193
beauty and fitness. *See* body;
    dieting; eyes; face; feet;
    gyms; hair; hands; jogging;
    makeup; piercings; skin;
    tattoos
beer belly, 277
beer bottle, opening without
    bottle opener, 248
beer-can chicken explosion, 250
Bell's Palsy, 50
bifocals, adjusting to, 276
Bigfoot sighting, 191
bikes. *See* cycling
binging, while dieting, 61
birds
    caught in hair, 43
    droppings in hair, 45
    as intruders in house, 97
    as pets, 110

ABOUT THE AUTHORS

Joshua Piven often ponders the meaning of life. What are we here for? What's it all about? What's the best way to clean up messy food spills? When not pondering, he is authoring the *Worst-Case Scenario Survival Handbook* series with David Borgenicht. He lives in Philadelphia.

David Borgenicht is a writer, editor, and thrill-seeker who prides himself on the fact that he is still alive. He is the co-author, along with Joshua Piven, of all of the books in *The Worst-Case Scenario Survival Handbook* series. He lives in Philadelphia with his wife and children, and his goal is to live forever—so far, so good.

Brenda Brown is an illustrator and cartoonist whose work has been published in many books and publications, including *The Worst-Case Scenario Survival Handbook* series, *Esquire*, *Reader's Digest*, *USA Weekend*, *21st Century Science & Technology*, the *Saturday Evening Post*, and the *National Enquirer*. Her website is http://webtoon.com.

Check out www.worstcasescenarios.com for updates, new scenarios, and more! Because you just never know . . .

Acknowledgments

Josh thanks all the usual suspects, his co-author Dave; editors Melissa, Jay, and Steve; illustrator Brenda; and all the other Worst-Case "lifers."

This book, like life itself, wouldn't have been possible without the hard work, participation, and occasional nagging of lots of other people. In particular, David would like to thank his editors—Jay Schaefer, Steve Mockus, and Melissa Wagner—designer Frances J. Soo Ping Chow, writer Piers Marchant, illustrator Brenda Brown, and the entire staffs at Quirk Books and Chronicle Books. Life wouldn't be worth living without you.

THE FIRST OF THE WORST

⚠ 3 million copies in print

⚠ Translated into 27 languages

⚠ International best-seller

"An armchair guide for the anxious."
—*USA Today*

"The book to have when the killer bees arrive."
—*The New Yorker*

"Nearly 180 pages of immediate action drills for when everything goes to hell in a handbasket."
—*Soldier of Fortune*

"This is a really nifty book."
—*Forbes*

A BOOK FOR EVERY DISASTER